HEART HEALTHY

COOKBOOK FOR BEGINNERS

1500 Days of Delicious and Easy-To-Follow Recipes
to Lower Your Blood Pressure and Cholesterol Level

MELISSA WESTWOOD

TABLE OF CONTENTS

Introduction

A healthy diet is an essential part of living a healthy life. Eating a diet that is good for your heart can lower your risk of heart disease and other health problems like high blood pressure and diabetes.

A heart-healthy diet has many different parts, but some of the most important things to focus on are eating a lot of fruits and vegetables, cutting back on saturated and trans fats, and choosing lean sources of protein.

What to Eat and What Not to Eat

We are what we eat, which is no mystery. Food has a direct impact on both our physical and emotional health. That's why it's important to consider what we put in our bodies. There are some foods that are widely thought to be healthier than others, even if there are no hard-and-fast rules on what to eat and what to avoid.

A vital food for our bodies is protein. It produces enzymes and hormones, aids in tissue growth and repair, and gives our DNA structure. Meat, poultry, fish, eggs, dairy products, beans, nuts, and seeds are all the best sources of protein.

It's critical to select protein-rich foods that are low in cholesterol and saturated fat. Good options include lean meats, skinless chicken, fish, tofu, lentils, and low-fat or fat-free dairy products.

It's crucial to keep in mind that we need to restrict our intake of some protein sources. Red and processed meats like bacon and sausage contain a lot of cholesterol and saturated fat and should only be consumed in moderation.

One nutrient that is frequently forgotten when it comes to eating for health is fiber. Everyone should strive to get roughly 25 grams of fiber every day because it is an essential component of a balanced diet.

Soluble and insoluble fibers are both available. When soluble fiber dissolves in water, a gel-like substance is produced that can aid in slowing down digestion and keeping you fuller for longer. Insoluble fiber helps to add weight to your stool, which can aid with bowel regularity because it does not dissolve in water.

Fruits, vegetables, legumes, whole grains, nuts, and legume products are just a few examples of foods that contain fiber. Black beans, lentils, broccoli, Brussels sprouts, oats, chia seeds, and flaxseeds are a few examples of foods high in fiber. By simply substituting some refined carbs in your diet, you may easily add extra fiber to it.

Consuming enough fiber is essential for overall health and wellbeing. Fiber intake has been demonstrated to reduce the risk of obesity, type 2 diabetes, heart disease, and stroke. Additionally, fiber can help decrease cholesterol and maintain healthy blood sugar levels. So, bear it in mind the next time you prepare a meal or a snack.

It's best to stay as far away from added sugar as you can. Limiting sweetened foods and beverages like candy, cake, and soda is necessary to achieve this. Instead, choose naturally sweet meals like fruits and vegetables. If you do consume items with added sugar, make sure to counterbalance them with healthier foods to avoid overdosing on your body.

BREAKFAST

RECIPES

Spinach Omelet

Preparation time: 10 minutes   Cooking time: 5 minutes

Ingredients:

- 2 slices of whole grain bread
- 1 pc. of avocado
- smoked salmon, 4 oz
- to taste: salt and pepper
- lemon juice (optional)

Directions:

1. Toasted bread should be as crisp as you like.
2. Remove the avocado's pit, cut it in half, and ladle the flesh into a small bowl. Use a fork or a potato to mash it until it reaches your desired consistency.
3. Spread the mashed avocado on top of the toast.
4. Set the avocado on the top of the toast.
5. Drizzle some salt and pepper on top of the salmon.
6. Add some lemon juice on top (optional).

Nutrition: Calories: 216.2; Fat: 17.5g; Carbs: 1.2g; Protein: 12.7g

Roasted Vegetable and Egg Skillet

Preparation time: 5 minutes   Cooking time: 7 minutes

Ingredients:

- 1 tbsp. olive oil
- 3 cups sliced mixed vegetables (such as zucchini, mushrooms, onions, bell pepper)
- 1 tbsp. garlic powder
- Salt
- Black pepper
- 4 eggs
- 1/4 cup sliced fresh cilantro

Directions:

1. Turn on the grill. Heat the olive oil in a medium baking dish or broiler-safe pan.

2. Add the garlic powder and veggies. Add salt and pepper, then lightly toss to coat.

3. After about 2 minutes, stir the skillet and cook it for an additional 2 minutes under the broiler on the center oven shelf.

4. Bring the pan out of the oven, top with eggs, and put it back under the broiler.

5. Broil until cooked to your liking: for over easy eggs, about 2 to 3 minutes.

6. Watch closely as the eggs will cook quickly.

7. Divide the vegetable and egg mixture between two serving plates, top with the fresh cilantro, and serve immediately.

Nutrition: Calories: 242; Fat: 17g; Carbs: 14g; Protein: 14g

Lentil Asparagus Omelet

Preparation time: 15 minutes   Cooking time: 20 minutes

Ingredients:

- 4 eggs, whisked
- 1 tbsp. dried thyme
- 1/4 cup sliced onion
- 1 cup sliced asparagus (about half pound asparagus)

- 1/2 cup rinsed and drained legumes from a can
- 1/2 sliced grape tomatoes, for sprinkling
- 8 avocado slices, for topping (optional)

Directions:

1. In a bowl, set together the eggs and thyme. Bring them aside.

2. Put a little nonstick skillet on medium fire to preheat.

3. For 2-3 minutes after adding, attach the shallot and asparagus. Lentils are then added, and they are cooked through after another 2 minutes of cooking.

4. To stay warm, turn the thermostat down all the way.

5. Turn on the medium heat under a medium nonstick pan.

6. Add 1/2 of the eggs to the frying skillet and cook for 2 to 3 minutes after another whisking of the eggs.

7. Seal 1/2 of the eggs with half of the asparagus lentil concoction.

8. Fold the egg over the mixture and continue cooking for an additional 1 to 2 minutes.
9. Move the dish to a presentation plate.
10. To prepare the second omelet, repeat steps 1-4 with the remaining ingredients.
11. Sprinkle with the chopped tomatoes and avocado slices (if using) and serve promptly.

Nutrition: Calories: 242; Fat: 9g; Carbs: 22g; Protein: 19g:

Eggs in an Avocado

Preparation time: 15 minutes   Cooking time: 20 minutes

Ingredients:

- 1 large avocado, halved, pitted, and peeled
- Salt
- Freshly ground black pepper
- 1 tablespoon olive oil, divided

- 2 large eggs
- 3 or 4 tablespoons water
- 1/2 cup halved cherry tomatoes
- 1/4 cup chopped fresh chives

Directions:

1. Lay the avocado halves on a clean work surface, hollow side up.
2. Gently press the avocado down to slightly flatten the bottom so it will sit without tipping. (Keep the hollow part of the avocado intact to crack the eggs into later). Set with salt and pepper.
3. Heat 1/2 tbsp. of olive oil in a high sided skillet over medium high heat.
4. Add the avocado halves, hollow side up.
5. Let the avocado to seat for 1 minute.
6. Crack an egg into each hollow. Set the eggs with salt and pepper.
7. Pour 3 or 4 tbsp. of water into the bottom of the pan and cover the pan with a lid.
8. Bring the water to a simmer and let the eggs steam for 3 to 5 minutes, or until the egg whites have set and the yolks are firm (or set to your liking).

9. Meanwhile, in a bowl, merge together the tomatoes, chives, and rem
tablespoon of olive oil.

10. Set with salt and pepper.

11. Remove the egg-stuffed avocados to two serving plates. Top with the tomato and chive mixture and serve.

Nutrition: Calories: 346; Fat: 2g; Carbs: 11g; Protein: 9g

Shrimp Salad with Avocado

Preparation time: 10 minutes

Cooking time: 10 minutes

Ingredients:

- 1 lb. cooked and peeled shrimp
- One avocado, diced
- 1/4 cup minced red onion
- 1/4 cup minced celery

- 2 tbsp. sliced fresh cilantro
- 2 tbsp. mayonnaise
- 1 tbsp. citrus juice, fresh
- To taste: Salt and pepper

Directions:

1. Combine the shrimp, avocado, red onion, celery, and cilantro in a big bowl.
2. Set together the mayonnaise, lime juice, salt, and pepper in a small bowl.
3. Toss the shrimp mixture with the dressing after pouring it over it.
4. Serve chilled on a bed of lettuce or as a sandwich filling.

Nutrition: Calories: 469.5; Fat: 5.4g; Carbs: 3.6g; Protein: 32.3g

Peanut Butter Banana Oatmeal

Preparation time: 5 minutes

Cooking time: 10 minutes

Ingredients:

- A banana
- Half cup of rolled oats

- 1/2 cup milk or a substitute for milk
- Peanut butter, two tablespoons

- A spoonful of honey (optional)

Directions:

1. Peel and mash the banana in a small saucepan.
2. Stir together the oats, milk, and peanut butter in the pot.
3. Stirring occasionally, warm the mixture over medium heat until it achieves the required consistency. Optional: Stir in honey for added sweetness.

Nutrition: Calories: 369; Fat: 12g; Carbs: 31g; Protein: 11g

Creamy Millet Porridge with Berries

Preparation time: 5 minutes   Cooking time: 25 minutes

Ingredients:

- 2 cups of strawberries
- 1 tbsp. of maple syrup
- 1 1/2 cups of almond milk with added protein (or soy milk)
- 1/4 cup of sliced almonds
- 1 cup of millet
- 1 1/2 cups of water

Directions:

1. Set the oven to 375 degrees. Merge the maple syrup with the fruit. Roast the strawberries for 15-20 minutes, or until they are juicy and tender.
2. Place the millet in a medium saucepan over medium heat, and toast for 3 to 4 minutes, stirring occasionally, until fragrant and barely browned.
3. Take the food off the fire and let it cool slightly.
4. Grind the millet in a coffee grinder or mixer, and process until it is approximately split in half between grain and flour.
5. Bring together the millet, milk, and water in a medium saucepan over medium low heat.
6. Simmer, stirring frequently for 15 to 20 minutes, or until it has a texture of porridge, and the grain bits are soft. If the grain is not soft, add a bit more milk. If the grains are not soft, add a bit more milk and continue to process until the grains are tender.

7. Top with extra milk, chopped almonds, and roasted strawberries.

Nutrition: Calories: 561; Fat: 12g; Carbs: 8g; Protein: 16g

Apricot Granola with Fresh Fruit

Preparation time: 5 minutes   Cooking time: 5 minutes

Ingredients:

- 1/4 cup gluten-free rolled oats
- 2 tablespoons almonds
- 2 tablespoons walnuts
- 2 tablespoons ground flaxseed
- 3/4 tablespoon olive oil
- 1 tablespoon maple syrup
- Pinch ground cinnamon

- 1/4 cup chopped dried apricots
- 1 mango, peeled and chopped
- 3/4 cup fresh strawberries
- 1/2 cup fresh blueberries
- Nonfat dairy milk or plant-based milk, for topping

Directions:

1. Attach the oats, almonds, walnuts, and flaxseed to a small pan over medium heat.
2. Stir until the oats and nuts are warm and starting to brown, 3 to 4 minutes.
3. Set the olive oil into the pan and stir until mixed through.
4. Do the same with the maple syrup.
5. Add the cinnamon and stir, then add the dried apricots and mix until combined.
6. Set off the heat and let it cool.
7. Peel and chop the mango, wash and slice the strawberries, and wash the blueberries.
8. Portion the granola into two serving bowls and top with the fresh fruit and milk.
9. Enjoy immediately.

Nutrition: Calories: 378; Fat: 7g; Carbs: 4g; Protein: 8g

Smashed Peas, Avocado, and Egg Toast

Preparation time: 5 minutes

Cooking time: 10 minutes

Ingredients:

- 2 slices whole-grain bread
- 1/2 ripe avocado, sliced
- 1/4 cup peas (fresh or frozen and thawed)
- Salt

- Freshly ground black pepper
- 1/2 red onion, thinly sliced
- 1 hard-boiled egg, cut in half
- Fresh basil leaves, for garnish

Directions:

1. Toast the bread and set it aside.
2. Start by mashing half of an avocado in a small bowl.
3. Add the peas to the bowl and continue mashing until they are well combined with the avocado.
4. Add salt and pepper to taste.
5. Spread the avocado-pea mixture on each slice of toast.
6. Top equally with the remaining avocado slices, red onion slices, egg, and basil.
7. Enjoy immediately.

Nutrition: Calories: 22; Fat: 13g; Carbs: 22g; Protein: 8g

Coconut Milk Pudding

Preparation time: 5 minutes, plus 8 hours or overnight chilling time

Cooking time: 0 minutes

Ingredients:

- 1/2 cup chia seeds
- 2 cups light coconut milk
- 3 teaspoons honey, divided

- 1/4 cup sliced banana
- 1/4 cup fresh raspberries
- 1/2 tablespoon sliced almonds

- 1/2 tablespoon chopped walnuts
- 2 teaspoons unsweetened cocoa powder, divided

Directions:

1. Mix the chia seeds, coconut milk, and 2 teaspoons of honey together in a small bowl.
2. Portion into two glass Mason jars and refrigerate for 8 hours or overnight.
3. Remove the jars from the refrigerator and top each jar with half the banana, raspberries, almonds, walnuts, and cocoa.
4. Drizzle each jar with the remaining 1 tbsp. of honey, dividing it equally.

Nutrition: Calories: 732; Fat: 3g; Carbs: 1g; Protein: 13g

Apple Cinnamon Quinoa Breakfast Bowl

Preparation time: 5 minutes

Cooking time: 0 minutes

Ingredients:

- 1/2 cup uncooked quinoa
- 1 cup unsweetened vanilla or unflavored almond milk
- 1 or 2 cinnamon sticks
- 1/2 tbsp. ground cinnamon
- Salt

Toppings:

- 2 tbsp. sliced almonds
- 1 cup sliced apple
- 2 tbsp. hemp seeds
- Alternative sweeteners: stevia, brown sugar, honey

Directions:

1. Wash the quinoa thoroughly in a colander and drain.
2. Sprinkle the almond milk, cinnamon sticks, ground cinnamon, and salt to the small saucepan with the rice.
3. Return to a vigorous simmer, then adjust the heat to medium and cover. Keep 15 minutes simmering.
4. Turn off the heat and leave the quinoa in the skillet for 5 minutes so that the almond milk can be absorbed, and the quinoa can finish cooking.

5. Set the quinoa between two serving bowls.

6. Add half the almonds, apple, and hemp seeds to each bowl.

7. Add sweetener, if desired, and serve.

Nutrition: Calories: 360; Fat: 13g; Carbs: 14g; Protein: 14g

Spinach & Egg Scramble with Raspberries

Preparation time: 3 minutes   Cooking time: 10 minutes

Ingredients:

- 1 cup fresh spinach leaves
- 2 eggs
- Salt and pepper, to taste
- 1/4 cup raspberries
- 1 tablespoon olive oil or butter

Directions:

1. In a small skillet over medium heat, soothing the butter or olive oil.

2. Add the spinach leaves and simmer for two to three minutes, or until wilted.

3. Scramble eggs into the skillet and add pepper and salt to it.

4. Use a spatula to scramble the eggs and spinach together until the eggs are cooked through, about 2-3 minutes.

5. Gently fold in the raspberries into the scramble, being careful not to crush them.

6. Serve immediately.

Nutrition: Calories: 296; Fat: 15.7g; Carbs: 20.9g; Protein: 17.8g

Carrot Baked Oatmeal

Preparation time: 15 minutes   Cooking time: 45 minutes

Ingredients:

- 2 cups of dried oats
- 1 cup chopped carrots
- 1/2 cup sliced walnuts
- 1/2 cup raisins
- 1 tsp. cinnamon
- 1/2 tsp. cardamom

- 1/4 tsp. salt
- 1 1/2 a cup of milk
- A half-cup maple syrup
- Two eggs
- 1 tsp. vanilla extract

Directions:

1. Prepare the oven for cooking, adjust the temperature setting to 350 degrees Fahrenheit or 175 degrees Celsius.
2. A 9x13-inch pastry pan should be greased.
3. Combine the oats, grated carrots, chopped walnuts, raisins, cinnamon, nutmeg, and salt in a sizable mixing dish.
4. In a different bowl, combine the milk, maple syrup, eggs, and vanilla essence.
5. Once all the ingredients are thoroughly combined, stir the wet components into the dry ones.
6. Spoon the prepped baking dish with the mixture inside.
7. Bake for 35 to 40 minutes, or until the surface is golden brown and the oats are cooked. If preferred, serve warm with more milk or yogurt.

Nutrition: Calories: 236; Fat: 18g; Carbs: 1g; Protein: 19g

Bagel Avocado Toast

Preparation time: 5 minutes   Cooking time: 5 minutes

Ingredients:

- One bagel, sliced in half and toasted
- One avocado, mashed
- Salt and pepper, to taste
- Optional toppings: cherry tomatoes, red onion, lemon juice, hot sauce

Directions:

1. Toast the bagel halves until they are crispy and golden brown.
2. Mash the avocado with a fork or a potato masher in a small bowl.
3. To flavor, add salt and pepper.

4. Spread the avocado on top of the toasted bagel halves in an even layer.

5. You also have the option to add extras like cherry tomatoes, red onions, lemon juice, or spicy sauce.

6. Deliver instantly and savor.

Nutrition: Calories: 230; Fat: 11g; Carbs: 30g; Protein: 6g

Southwestern Waffle

Preparation time: 10 minutes

Cooking time: 3 minutes

Ingredients:

- 1 and a half cups of all-purpose flour
- 1/2 cup cornmeal
- 2 teaspoons of baking powder
- 1/2 teaspoon salt
- 1/4 tsp. cayenne pepper
- 1 1/2 cup of milk
- Two eggs

- Two tbsp. melted butter
- 1/2 cup minced onion
- 1/2 cup sliced bell pepper
- 1/2 cup chopped jalapeno pepper
- 1/2 cup sliced cooked ham
- 1/2 cup grated cheddar cheese

Directions:

1. In a big dish, combine the flour, cornmeal, baking powder, salt, and cayenne pepper.

2. In a different dish, combine the milk, eggs, and melted butter.

3. Add the liquid components to the dry ones and stir just until combined.

4. Mix the diced onion, bell pepper, jalapeno pepper, cooked ham, and shredded cheddar cheese.

5. Warm up a waffle iron and grease it lightly.

6. Spoon the batter into a waffle oven and cook it in accordance with the maker's instructions.

7. You can top the waffles with sour cream, salsa, avocado, or anything else you like.

Nutrition: Calories: 207; Fat: 12g; Carbs: 17g; Protein: 9g

Pineapple-Grapefruit Detox Smoothie

Preparation time: 5 minutes   Cooking time: 10 minutes

Ingredients:

- 12 a grapefruit, segmented and trimmed
- Half-cup pineapple chunks
- 1/2 banana
- 1 cup spinach
- 1/2 cup water or coconut nectar

Directions:

1. Peel and segment the grapefruit and set aside.
2. Fill a blender with spinach, banana, pineapple pieces, and water or coconut water.
3. Add grapefruit segments to the blender.
4. Mix till fluid.
5. Pour into a glass and enjoy

Nutrition: Calories: 102; Fat:0.2g; Carbs: 25.2g; Protein: 2g

Pistachio & Peach Toast

Preparation time: 5 minutes   Cooking time: 5 minutes

Ingredients:

- One slice of whole-grain bread
- 1/4 avocado, mashed
- 1/4 ripe peach, thinly sliced
- 1 tbsp chopped pistachios
- 1 tsp honey
- Salt and pepper to taste

Directions:

1. Toasted bread should be done to the desired crisp.
2. Spread mashed avocado on the toast.
3. Arrange the peach slices on the top of avocado.
4. Sprinkle chopped pistachios on top of the peaches.
5. Drizzle honey on top of the toast.
6. Add pepper and salt to flavor when seasoning.

Nutrition: Calories: 193; Fat: 6g; Carbs: 29g; Protein: 8.2g

Overnight Matcha Oats with Berries

Preparation time: 5 minutes   Cooking time: 15 minutes

Ingredients:

- Half a cup rolled oats
- 1/2 cup of almond milk
- 1/2 cup of water
- 1 tsp. of Matcha powder
- 1 tbsp. of honey
- 1/4 cup of mixed berries (fresh or frozen)

Directions:

1. In a mason jar or airtight container, combine oats, almond milk, water, matcha powder, and honey.
2. Mix everything thoroughly.
3. Add in the mixed berries and give it a final stir.
4. Cover and refrigerate overnight.
5. Give the oats a good stir in the morning and eat them cold or heat them up in the microwave for a warm breakfast.
6. You can add some nuts or seeds, like chia seeds, flax seeds, or chopped almonds, for added texture and nutrition.

Nutrition: Calories: 373; Fat: 1g; Carbs: 52g; Protein: 7g

Strawberry Peach Smoothie

Preparation time: 5 minutes   Cooking time: 5 minutes

Ingredients:

- 1 cup chilled strawberries
- One ripe peach, peeled and sliced
- 1/2 cup Greek yogurt
- 1/2 cup orange juice
- One tbsp. of honey (optional)

Directions:

1. Blend the frozen strawberries, diced peach, honey, Greek yogurt, and orange juice in a mixer (if using).
2. Blend at high speed until velvety and smooth.
3. Pour into a glass and serve immediately.
4. You can add some ice cubes if you want a thicker consistency.

Nutrition: Calories: 221; Fat: 1g; Carbs: 48g; Protein: 9g

Breakfast Parfait

Preparation time: 10 minutes   Cooking time: 0 minutes

Ingredients:

- 1 cup of unflavored Greek yogurt.
- 1/2 cup granola
- 1/2 cup fresh berries (such as strawberries, blueberries, or raspberries)

Directions:

1. Start by adding 1/4 cup of yogurt to the bottom of a parfait glass or container.
2. Add a layer of granola on top of the yogurt.
3. Place fruit on top of the granola layer.
4. Add the leftover yogurt, granola, and berries and layer again.

5. Enjoy immediately, or chill in the refrigerator for a few minutes before serving.

Nutrition: Calories: 212; Fat: 3g; Carbs: 41g; Protein: 9g

Almond Butter & Roasted Grape Toast

Preparation time: 10 minutes

Cooking time: 20 minutes

Ingredients:

- Two slices of bread
- Two tablespoons of almond butter

- 1/2 cup of red grapes
- One tablespoon of olive oil
- Salt and pepper to taste

Directions:

1. Turn on the oven at 425°F. Spread the almond butter on the bread slices.
2. Garnish the grapes on a baking tray with salt, pepper, and olive oil.
3. Roast the grapes in the oven for 8-10 minutes or until they start to burst.
4. Take the grapes out of the oven and allow them to settle just a little.
5. Toast the bread slices in the oven for two to three minutes, or until they are golden brown, by placing them on a baking sheet with almond butter.
6. Remove the toast from the oven and top it with the roasted grapes. Serve warm.

Nutrition: Calories: 219; Fat: 10g; Carbs: 28g; Protein: 7g

Healthy Bread Pudding

Preparation time: 30 minutes

Cooking time: 45 minutes

Ingredients:

- Four slices whole wheat bread, cut into cubes
- 2 cups of low-fat milk

- Two eggs
- 1/4 cup honey
- 1 tsp vanilla extract

Directions:

1. The oven should be set to 350 degrees Fahrenheit (175 degrees C). Grease a baking dish that holds 1 cup.
2. Arrange bread cubes in the prepared dish.
3. In a medium mixing dish, merge the milk, eggs, honey, cinnamon, vanilla extract, and salt. Pour mixture over bread cubes. Stir in raisins if desired.
4. Bake for 45 to 50 minutes, or until the center is firm, in a preheated oven.
5. Once ready. Serve the dish while it is still warm or let it cool down to room temperature before serving. You can add other ingredients, such as nuts, dried fruits, and spices, to make it more flavorful.

Nutrition: Calories: 157; Fat: 5g; Carbs: 24g; Protein: 6g

Muesli with Raspberries

Preparation time: 20 minutes   Cooking time: 15 minutes

Ingredients:

- 1 cup rolled oats
- 1/2 cup raspberries
- 1/4 cup chopped nuts (such as almonds, hazelnuts, or pecans)
- 1/4 cup dried fruit (such as raisins, cranberries, or apricots)
- 1/4 cup honey or maple syrup
- 1/2 cup milk or yogurt

Directions:

1. In a big dish, combine the oats, raspberries, nuts, and dried fruit.
2. In a second small bowl, combine the milk or yoghurt with the honey or maple syrup.
3. Pour liquid mixture over the oat mixture and stir until everything is well mixed.
4. Wrap it up and put it in the fridge for at least 30 minutes or overnight.
5. Serve the muesli with additional milk or yogurt and fresh raspberries, if desired..

Nutrition: Calories: 288; Fat: 6.6g; Carbs: 51g; Protein: 13g

Cannellini Bean & Herbed Ricotta Toast

Preparation time: 5 minutes   Cooking time: 5 minutes

Ingredients:

- One can of cannellini beans, drained and rinsed
- 1/2 cup of ricotta cheese
- 1 tbsp of chopped fresh herbs (such as parsley, basil, or thyme)
- Salt and pepper to taste
- One loaf of sourdough bread, sliced
- Olive oil for brushing
- Optional: red pepper flakes, lemon zest, or grated Parmesan cheese for topping

Directions:

1. Set the oven temperature to 375°F (190°C).
2. In a medium bowl, mash the cannellini beans with a fork or potato masher.
3. Stir in the ricotta cheese, herbs, salt, and pepper.
4. After brushing the bread pieces with olive oil, arrange them on a baking sheet.
5. Spread the bean mixture over the slices of bread. Optional toppings include shredded Parmesan cheese, lemon zest, or red pepper flakes.
6. Bake the bread and bean mixture for 10 to 15 minutes, or until they are heated through. Serve hot.

Nutrition: Calories: 320; Fat: 9g; Carbs: 42g; Protein: 15g

Egg Tartine

Preparation time: 10 minutes   Cooking time: 20 minutes

Ingredients:

- Four slices of bread (sourdough or baguette)
- Four eggs
- Four slices of bacon or pancetta
- Salt and pepper

- Arugula or other greens (optional)
- Butter (for spreading)
- Parmesan cheese (optional)

Directions:

1. Preheat the broiler. In a skillet, fry the bacon or pancetta until it is crispy. Remove, then dry off with paper napkins.
2. Butter each piece of bread on the outside.
3. Place the bread, butter-side-up, on a baking sheet and broil for 1-2 minutes or until lightly toasted.
4. Crack an egg onto each slice of toast, careful not to break the yolk. Sprinkle with salt and pepper.
5. Broil for an extra 2-3 minutes, or until the egg yolks have reached the desired level of firmness.
6. Top each toast with crispy bacon or pancetta and arugula or greens. Grated Parmesan may be added, if preferred. Serve immediately.

Nutrition: Calories: 184; Fat: 3g; Carbs: 14g; Protein: 10g

Candied Apples

Preparation time: 10 minutes

Cooking time: 30 minutes

Ingredients:

- 6 Granny Smith apples
- Six wooden sticks
- 2 cups of granulated sugar
- 1 cup of light corn syrup
- 1 cup of water
- red food coloring (optional)
- 1/4 teaspoon of cinnamon (optional

Directions:

1. Cover a baking pan with silicone mat or parchment paper. Put a stick of wood in the end of the stem of each apple.

2. In a small pot, merge the sugar, corn syrup, and water. Stirring the liquid will remove all of the sugar.

3. After the combination comes to a boil, reduce the heat to medium-low, lid, and simmer the mixture for approximately 10 minutes.

4. If desired, add a few drops of red food coloring or a sprinkle of cinnamon to the mixture.

5. Dip each apple into the mixture and turn it to make sure it is covered evenly. Let any extra liquid drip off, and then put the apples on the baking sheet that has been set up. Wait at least 30 minutes before serving the apples so they can settle and harden.

Nutrition: Calories: 237; Fat: 0g; Carbs: 63g; Protein: 0g

Tofu Scramble

Preparation time: 10 minutes   Cooking time: 20 minutes

Ingredients:

- 1 block of firm tofu
- One tablespoon of olive oil
- 1/2 onion, diced
- 1/2 bell pepper, diced
- 2 cloves of garlic, minced
- 1/4 teaspoon of turmeric
- 1/4 teaspoon of cumin
- 1/4 teaspoon of salt
- 1/4 teaspoon of pepper
- Two tablespoons of nutritional yeast (optional)
- Two tablespoons of chopped fresh parsley or cilantro (optional)

Directions:

1. The tofu should be drained and pressed to remove excess moisture. Divide it into manageable pieces.

2. Heat the oil in a skillet over medium heat. When the veggies are soft, add the onion, garlic, and bell pepper and cook for about 5 minutes.

3. Stir together the broken tofu, turmeric, cumin, salt, and pepper in the pan. Cook the tofu for about 5 minutes, or until it is thoroughly cooked.

4. Once the tofu is golden and crispy, add the nutritional yeast, if using, and mix.

5. Turn off the fire and stir in the cilantro or parsley that has been finely chopped.

6. Serve immediately and enjoy with toast, avocado, or any side of your choice.

Nutrition: Calories: 212; Fat: 15.1g; Carbs: 7.1g; Protein: 16.4g

Raspberry Mousse

Preparation time: 25 minutes   Cooking time: 10 minutes

Ingredients:

- 2 cups of fresh raspberries
- 1/4 cup of granulated sugar
- Two tablespoons of water
- Two teaspoons of unflavored gelatin powder
- 1 cup of heavy cream
- 1/4 cup of powdered sugar
- One teaspoon of vanilla extract

Directions:

1. In a medium saucepan, mix together the raspberries, granulated sugar, and water. Cook over medium heat, occasionally stirring, until the raspberries are soft and the mixture is thickened about 10-15 minutes.

2. Take the mixture off the heat and pour it through a fine-mesh sieve to get rid of the seeds. Toss the seeds and let the raspberry puree cool to room temperature.

3. Put the gelatin powder on top of two tablespoons of cold water in a small bowl and let it sit for five minutes to soften.

4. Heat the gelatin mixture over low heat in a medium saucepan until it is completely dissolved. Take it off the heat and let it cool down a bit.

5. Heavy cream, powdered sugar, and vanilla extract are mixed together in a large bowl until stiff peaks form.

6. Gently fold the raspberry puree and the cooled gelatin mixture into the whipped cream until well combined. Pour the mousse into individual serving glasses or a large bowl and chill in the refrigerator for at least 2-3 hours or until set.

7. Serve chilled and enjoy with fresh raspberries or whipped cream on top.

Nutrition: Calories: 169; Fat: 11g; Carbs: 17g; Protein: 2g

Summer Berry Parfait with Yogurt

Preparation time: 10 minutes   Cooking time: 10 minutes

Ingredients:

- 2 cups mixed berries (strawberries, blueberries, raspberries, blackberries)
- 1 cup plain Greek yogurt
- 1/2 cup granola

Directions:

1. Wash and hull the berries. Cut the strawberries into small pieces.
2. Arrange the granola, yogurt, and berries in a glass or dish.
3. Repeat layering until all ingredients are used.
4. Either serve right away or cover and chill the dish until you're ready to serve it.
5. You can add honey or maple syrup to sweeten the yogurt or toasted coconut flakes for extra crunch. Cover the bowl and put it in the fridge for at least 30 minutes to let the flavors mix.

Nutrition: Calories: 521; Fat: 14g; Carbs: 87g; Protein: 18g

LUNCH RECIPES

Chicken and Pesto Sourdough Sandwich

Preparation time: 10 minutes

Cooking time: 55-60 minutes

Ingredients:

- 2 pairs of sourdough bread
- 2 tbsp. pesto
- 4 oz. cooked, cut chicken breast

- 1/4 cup mozzarella cheese, shredded
- 1/4 cup sliced sun-dried tomatoes
- To taste: salt and pepper

Directions:

1. Spread pesto on one side of each slice of bread.
2. Top one piece of bread with the sliced chicken, melted mozzarella cheese, and thinly sliced sun-dried tomatoes.
3. To flavor, add salt and pepper to the mixture.
4. Place the other piece of bread on top, with the pesto side facing in.
5. Heat it up a skillet on medium-high heat.
6. Attach the sandwich in the skillet and toast the bread and melt the cheese for 2 to 3 minutes on both sides.

Nutrition: Calories: 390; Fat: 13g; Carbs: 31g; Protein: 37g

Turkey and Spinach Rice Bowl

Preparation time: 5 minutes

Cooking time: 20 minutes

Ingredients:

- 1 lb ground turkey
- One teaspoon of olive oil
- One onion, diced
- Two cloves of garlic, minced
- One teaspoon of ground cumin
- Salt and pepper, to taste

- 2 cups cooked white rice
- 2 cups fresh spinach leaves
- 1/4 cup diced tomatoes
- 1/4 cup crumbled feta cheese
- Two tablespoons chopped fresh parsley (optional)

Directions:

1. Prepare the olive oil by heating it in a sizable skillet over medium-high heat. When the chopped turkey is browned, add it and stir for about 5 minutes. Remove any extra fat.

2. To the skillet, attach the onion, garlic, cumin, salt, and pepper. Cook for roughly five minutes or until the onion turns clear.

3. Mix in the cooked rice, tomatoes, spinach, and feta cheese. Process for about 2 minutes, or until the spinach has turned limp.

4. If you want, you can add fresh parsley to the top of each bowl.

Nutrition: Calories: 304; Fat: 6g; Carbs: 24g; Protein: 20g

Two-Mushroom Barley Soup

Preparation time: 10 minutes   Cooking time: 20 minutes

Ingredients:

- 2 teaspoons olive oil
- 1 cup sliced carrots
- 1 cup diced onion
- 1/2 cup chopped celery
- 4 cups chopped button mushrooms
- 1 cup chopped shiitake mushrooms
- 2 garlic cloves, crushed
- 11/2 teaspoons chopped fresh thyme
- 1/8 teaspoon salt
- 1/8 teaspoon freshly ground black pepper
- 2 cups nonfat milk or plant-based milk
- 1 cup water
- 1/3 cup quick-cooking barley

Directions:

1. In a big pot over medium heat, prepare the olive oil. Add the shiitake and button mushrooms, along with the carrots, onion, celery, garlic, and thyme. Three minutes of stirring should be enough to get the veggies to start releasing some of their juices. Change up the heat to medium-high and simmer for an additional 3 minutes, stirring frequently, or until most of the liquid has evaporated.

2. Add the milk, water, and barley. Boil the concoction while frequently stirring it. Decrease the heat and simmer, stirring occasionally, for about 15 minutes, or until the vegetables and barley are tender.

3. Spoon into plates and devour right away.

Nutrition: Calories: 31; Fat: 6g; Carbs: 5.4g; Protein: 18g

Hearty White Bean and Kale Soup

Preparation time: 10 minutes   Cooking time: 30 minutes

Ingredients:

- 2 tbsp. of freshly squeezed lemon juice
- 1 cup of well-sliced onion
- 1/2 cup of sliced red bell pepper
- 1 tbsp. of sliced fresh rosemary leaves
- 1 bay leaf
- 1/4 cup of sliced celery
- 4 garlic cloves, thinly sliced

- 1 can of white beans
- 2 cups packed, stemmed, and finely sliced of kale
- Salt
- 3 cups of low-sodium vegetable broth
- 1 tbsp. of olive oil
- Freshly ground black pepper

Directions:

1. In a shallow skillet over medium-high heat, warm the olive oil. Add the rosemary, onion, bell pepper, celery, and garlic. The shallots and garlic should soften but not brown after 4 minutes of frequent stirring.

2. Include the legumes, broth, and bay leaf. Come to a boil, lower the heat, and stew for 10 minutes.

3. Toss in the kale and cook it for another 5 minutes or so, or until it is fully wilted.

4. Sprinkle with salt and pepper.

5. Drizzle the lemon juice, then serve right away.

Nutrition: Calories: 531; Fat: 10g; Carbs: 79g; Protein: 34g

Chicken and Rice Stew

Preparation time: 20 minutes

Cooking time: 50 minutes

Ingredients:

- 3 ounces chicken breast, cut into cubes
- 1/2 cup of sliced carrots
- 1 tbsp. of sliced fresh parsley
- 1/3 cup of dry long grain brown rice
- 2 garlic cloves, chopped
- 2 cups of stemmed and deveined kale

- 2 tbsp. of lime juice
- 1/2 cups of low sodium chicken broth
- 1/4 cup of sliced onion
- 1/4 cup of sliced onion
- 1/4 cup of sliced celery
- 1/8 tbsp. of dried thyme
- 1 bay leaf

Directions:

1. Combine the chicken broth, onion, garlic, celery, carrots, parsley, pepper, thyme, and the bay leaf in a large saucepan or Dutch oven. Set to a boil. Set the heat to low and simmer for 10 to 15 minutes, or until the onion and celery start to mellow.
2. Place the chicken and rice into the simmering broth and cook until the rice is soft and the chicken has been completely cooked and no longer pink in the middle.
3. Detach the bay leaf and stir in the kale and lime juice. Serve hot.

Nutrition: Calories: 531; Fat: 10g; Carbs: 79g; Protein: 34g

Fried Chicken Bowl

Preparation time: 10 minutes

Cooking time: 10 minutes

Ingredients:

- 1 lb. boneless, chicken thighs
- 1 cup of all-purpose flour
- 2 tsp. paprika

- 1 tsp. of garlic powder
- 1 tsp. of onion powder
- To taste: Salt and pepper,

- p of buttermilk
- or frying
- ps of cooked white rice
- p of frozen corn, thawed
- 1/4 cup sliced tomatoes

- 1/4 cup chopped scallions
- Optional hot sauce or barbecue marinade for dipping

Directions:

1. Merge the flour, paprika, garlic powder, salt onion powder and pepper in a shallow dish.
2. Set the buttermilk into a dish on its own.
3. Warmth the oil in a pan over medium-high heat.
4. Soak the chicken thighs in the buttermilk, and then roll them in the flour brew.
5. Slowly place the chicken in the pan and cook for 3 to 4 minutes on every side, until the chicken is fully cooked and golden brown.
6. Take the chicken out of the pan and place it on a plate lined with paper towels to drain.
7. Mix the cooked rice, corn, tomatoes, and scallions together in a large bowl.
8. Detach the chicken from the pan and set it on a plate covered in paper napkins to allow it to drain. If you want, you can serve it with hot sauce or barbecue sauce.

Nutrition: Calories: 592; Fat: 13g; Carbs: 49g; Protein: 14g

Baked Mustard-Lime Chicken

Preparation time: 10 minutes

Cooking time: 20 minutes

Ingredients:

- 1/4 tbsp. black pepper
- 2 garlic cloves, minced
- 1/4 cup of freshly squeezed lime juice
- 1/4 cup of sliced fresh cilantro
- 1/8 tbsp. of salt

- 1/2 tbsp. of olive oil
- 1/2 tbsp. of chili powder
- 2 tbsp. of Dijon mustard
- 2 skinless, boneless chicken breasts

Directions:

1. Establish the oven's temperature to 350° F.
2. In a food processor, mix the lime juice, cilantro, garlic, mustard, olive oil, chili powder, salt and pepper by pulsing the ingredients.
3. Arrange the chicken breasts in a 7 by 11-inch glass baking tray that can withstand the oven. Place the poultry in the refrigerator for a minimum of 15 minutes or up to 6 hours after spreading the marinade over it.
4. Microwave for 18-20 minutes, uncovered, or till an instant-read thermometer reads 165°F. Provide right away.

Nutrition: Calories: 189; Fat: 5g; Carbs: 4g; Protein: 27g

Easy Keto Korean Beef with Cauli Rice

Preparation time: 10 minutes   Cooking time: 10 minutes

Ingredients:

- 1 lb. ground beef
- 2 tbsp. olive oil
- 1/4 cup of soy sauce
- 2 cloves of garlic, sliced
- 1 tsp. grated ginger
- 1 tsp. sesame oil

- A half tsp. red pepper flakes (optional)
- to taste: Salt and pepper
- 1/4 cup green onions, thinly minced
- 1 head of cauliflower, grated or sliced into small florets

Directions:

1. Place the olive oil in a pan or skillet set to medium-high heat.
2. Attach the ground beef and process for about 5 minutes. Get rid of any extra fat.
3. Merge the soy sauce, garlic, sesame oil, ginger, red pepper flakes, salt, and pepper in a small dish with a whisk.
4. Pour the sauce over the beef and stir to cover it. Continue to stew for a further 2-3 minutes, or until the sauce thickens.
5. Take the skillet off the heat and add the green onions.
6. Pulse the florets of cauliflower in a food processor until they look like rice.

nmer the cauliflower rice in a different skillet until it is cooked through.
ve the beef mixture over the cauliflower rice.

Calories: 297; Fat: 19g; Carbs: 9g; Protein: 22g

Chicken with Mushroom Sauce

Preparation time: 5 minutes   Cooking time: 15 minutes

Ingredients:

- 1 tablespoon olive oil, divided
- 2 (6-ounce) skinless, boneless chicken breasts
- 1/4 teaspoon salt, divided
- 1/8 teaspoon freshly ground black pepper
- 1/4 cup chopped shallots
- 4 ounces button mushrooms, sliced

- 1 portobello mushroom, sliced
- 2 garlic cloves, minced
- 1/4 cup dry white wine, cooking wine, or low-sodium broth
- 1 teaspoon flour
- 1/2 cup water
- 2 teaspoons minced fresh thyme

Directions:

1. Warmth in a sizable nonstick pan over medium-high heat, apply 1 teaspoon of olive oil and swirl to coat. Add pepper and 1/8 teaspoon of salt to the poultry. An instant-read thermometer should measure 165°F once frying the chicken for about a minute on each side in the skillet. Chicken should be placed on a serving dish and kept warm.

2. To the skillet, add the shallots and mushrooms and cook stirring periodically for about 4 minutes or until browned. Add the garlic and beat constantly for a minute. Add the wine and stir, scraping the bottom of the pan to get out any browned pieces. Bring to a boil, then stew until the juice is almost gone.

3. Sprinkle the mushroom mixture with the remaining 1/8 teaspoon of salt and the flour and cook for about 30 seconds, stirring constantly. Use the water tp a boil while the pan is attached. Continue to cook for 2 more minutes, or until slightly

viscous. Take out the skillet from the heat, then incorporate in the thyme and the remaining 2 teaspoons of olive oil. Drizzle the meat with the sauce.

Nutrition: Calories: 329; Fat: 10g; Carbs: 12g; Protein: 44g

Asian Chicken Lettuce Wraps

Preparation time: 5 minutes   Cooking time: 20 minutes

Ingredients:

- 1/2 tbsp. of freshly grated lime zest
- 4 Boston lettuce leaves
- 1/2 tbsp. rice vinegar
- 1/2 tbsp. low-sodium soy sauce
- 1/2 tbsp. olive oil
- 2 tbsp. sliced peanuts
- 1 lime, cut into 4 wedges
- 1/2 tbsp. dark sesame oil
- 1 tbsp. chili sauce

- 1 garlic clove, sliced
- 2 (6 ounce) skinless, boneless chicken breasts
- Olive oil nonstick cooking spray
- 1 tbsp skinned and grated fresh ginger
- 1/2 cup fresh mint leaves
- 1/2 cup bean sprouts
- 1/2 cup sliced red bell pepper

Directions:

1. Gather together the olive and sesame oils, vinegar, soy sauce, chili sauce, ginger, lime zest, and garlic in a small dish. Reserve 1 tablespoon of the mixture.
2. Add the remaining mixture to a large resealable bag.
3. Add the chicken breasts, seal the bag, and marinate 1 hour, turning occasionally.
4. Take the poultry out of the bag, then throw away the marinade.
5. Set a sizable grill skillet that is nonstick to medium-high heat.
6. Spray some cooking spray on the skillet.
7. Add the chicken and cook it, turning once midway through, for 12 minutes, or until the thermometer registers 165°F.
8. Let it stand for 5 minutes before thinly slicing.
9. Divide the chicken among the lettuce leaves.

10. Top each lettuce leaf with mint, sprouts, bell pepper, and 1/2 teaspoon of the reserved dressing.

11. Garnish with the chopped peanuts, wrap like a burrito, and serve with the lime wedges.

Nutrition: Calories: 346; Fat: 14g; Carbs: 11g; Protein: 45g

Pan-Seared Pork and Fried Tomato Salad

Preparation time: 20 minutes   Cooking time: 20 minutes

Ingredients:

- Four boneless pork chops
- Salt and pepper to taste
- 2 cups all-purpose flour
- Two eggs, lightly beaten
- 2 cups breadcrumbs
- 2 cups vegetable oil for frying
- Four green tomatoes, sliced
- 1/4 cup chopped fresh parsley

- Two tablespoons of Dijon mustard
- Two tablespoons honey
- Two tablespoons of white wine vinegar
- 1/4 cup olive oil
- Salt and pepper to taste

Directions:

1. Add salt and pepper to the pork chops. In separate shallow dishes, set out the flour, eggs, and breadcrumbs.
2. Coat the pork chops with flour, then dunk them in the beaten eggs before rolling them in the breadcrumbs.
3. Arrange the vegetable oil in a sizable skillet and heat it over medium-high heat. The pork chunks should be fried for two to three minutes on each side, or until they're thoroughly cooked. Use paper towels as a drain.
4. Fry the green tomatoes in the same pan for 2 to 3 minutes on each side, or till they turn into golden brown. Use paper towels as a drain.
5. Whisk together the parsley, Dijon mustard, honey, white wine vinegar, olive oil, salt, and pepper in a small bowl.

6. Put the pork chops, dressing, and fried green tomatoes in a sizable salad platter.

7. Toss gently to coat.

Nutrition: Calories: 354; Fat: 16g; Carbs: 22g; Protein: 29g

Bourbon Steak

Preparation time: 10 minutes   Cooking time: 8 minutes

Ingredients:

- 2 (8 oz) steaks (such as ribeye or strip)
- Salt and pepper, to taste
- 2 tablespoons of olive oil
- 2 cloves of garlic, minced
- 1/4 cup of bourbon

- 1/4 cup of beef broth
- 1 tablespoon of unsalted butter
- 1 tablespoon of fresh thyme, chopped (optional)

Directions:

1. Ensure that your grill or cast iron skillet is preheated to high heat before you begin cooking.
2. Preheat your grill or cast iron skillet to high heat and set the steaks with salt and pepper. In the grill pan, warmth up the olive oil. Add the steaks to the pan and cook for 2 to 3 minutes per side for medium-rare or longer for well done.
3. Take the steaks off the pan and let them rest.
4. In the same pan, attach garlic and cook it for 1 minute.
5. Remove the pan from heat and carefully add the bourbon. Use a long-handled lighter or match to ignite the bourbon. Allow the flames to die down.
6. Resume heating the pan and add the beef broth. Process for 2-3 minutes, or until the sauce has thickened.
7. Set the pan off the heat and stir in the butter.
8. Place the rested steak back into the pan, spooning the sauce over the steak.
9. Garnish with fresh thyme, if desired, and serve immediately.

10. Note: It is important to use a good quality bourbon for this recipe, as the alcohol taste will come through in the final dish. And you can also add some mushrooms or shallots to the sauce for more flavor.

Nutrition: Calories: 368; Fat: 15g; Carbs: 16g; Protein: 27g

Fish Chowder Sheet Pan Bake

Preparation time: 15 minutes   Cooking time: 15 minutes

Ingredients:

- 4-6 fish fillets (cod, halibut, or haddock)
- 1/2 tsp. Old Bay seasoning
- To taste: Salt and pepper
- 1/4 cup of all-purpose flour
- 2 tbsp. butter
- 1 medium onion, sliced
- 2 cloves garlic, diced
- 2 cups chicken or fish broth
- 1 cup of heavy cream
- 1 cup of sliced potatoes
- 1 cup of frozen corn
- 1/4 cup of sliced fresh parsley

Directions:

1. Prepare the oven to 425 F (220 C). Grease a sheet pan.
2. Flavor the fish fillets with Old Bay seasoning, salt, and pepper.
3. Place flour in a shallow dish. Dredge fish fillets in flour, shaking off any excess.
4. In a large skillet, melt butter over medium heat. Add the onion and garlic and cook them until they are soft.
5. Stir in broth, cream, potatoes, corn, and parsley. Set to a simmer.
6. Place the fish fillets on the prepared sheet pan and pour the sauce over the fish.
7. Bake for 15-20 minutes or until fish is well done and potatoes are tender.
8. Set with fresh parsley and serve hot.

Nutrition: Calories: 412; Fat: 18g; Carbs: 28g; Protein: 33g

Maple Salmon

Preparation time: 10 minutes

Cooking time: 20 minutes

Ingredients:

- 4-6 oz. salmon fillets
- To taste: Salt and pepper
- 2 tbsp. olive oil
- 2 tbsp. maple syrup
- 2 cloves of garlic, sliced

- 1 tsp. Dijon mustard
- 1 tsp. citrus juice
- 2 tbsp. sliced fresh parsley (optional)

Directions:

1. Turn on the oven and adjust the temperature to 400°F (200°C).
2. Salt and pepper both sides of the salmon fillets.
3. Mix the olive oil, maple syrup, garlic, lemon juice, and mustard together in a small bowl with a whisk.
4. Drizzle the maple sauce over the salmon fillets that were laid in a baking tray.
5. Bake the salmon for 12 to 15 minutes, or until it's completely done and crusty.
6. Take it out of the oven and, if you want, top it with fresh parsley.

Nutrition: Calories: 265; Fat: 12g; Carbs: 14g; Protein: 23g

Hawaiian Chop Steaks

Preparation time: 5 minutes

Cooking time: 15 minutes

Ingredients:

- 2 lbs sirloin steak, cut into 4 pieces
- 1/4 cup soy sauce
- 1/4 cup brown sugar
- 2 tbsp olive oil
- 2 cloves garlic, minced

- 1 tsp ginger, grated
- 1/2 tsp black pepper
- 1/4 cup pineapple juice
- 1/4 cup green onions, chopped
- 1/4 cup cilantro, chopped

Directions:

1. Mix soy sauce, brown sugar, olive oil, garlic, ginger, black pepper, pineapple juice, green onions, and cilantro together in a shallow dish.

2. Add the pieces of steak and turn them to coat them all. Cover the meat and put it in the fridge for at least an hour or up to a day.

3. Set up the heat on a grill or grill pan.

4. Take the steak out of the marinade and throw away any extra marinade.

5. Grill the steaks for 3–4 minutes on each side, or until they reach the doneness you want.

6. Wait a few minutes before cutting the steaks and serving them.

7. Remarks: a pan or broiler can also be used if you don't have a grill.

8. For medium rare, cook for about 4-5 minutes per side, and for medium, cook for about 5-6 minutes per side.

Nutrition: Calories: 257; Fat: 11g; Carbs: 17g; Protein: 21g

Shrimp Capellini

Preparation time: 10 minutes   Cooking time: 30 minutes

Ingredients:

- 1 lb. of shrimp, peeled and sliced
- 8 oz. of capellini pasta
- 2 cloves of garlic, sliced
- 1/4 cup of white wine
- 1/4 cup of chicken or veggies broth
- 1 citrus, juiced
- 2 tbsp. of olive oil
- 2 tbsp. of butter
- To taste: Salt and pepper,
- Fresh parsley, sliced (optional for garnish)

Directions:

1. Bring a large pot of salted water to a boil. Follow the directions on the package to cook the capellini until it is al dente. Clean and store.

2. Adjust the stove to medium heat and warm up the olive oil in a pan. Warmth olive oil in a pan over medium heat. Attach sliced garlic and cook for about a minute, or until the garlic begins to smell nice.

1. Set the shrimp in the pan and process for about 2-3 minutes.

2. Take the shrimp out of the pan and put them on a plate.

3. In the same skillet, attach the white wine, lemon juice, chicken or vegetable broth, salt and pepper. Set the mixture to a simmer.

4. Attach the shrimp and capellini that have been done, as well as the butter, to the pan. Merge everything together until the sauce covers the pasta well. Cook for 1-2 minutes, or until the shrimp and pasta are warm. If you want, garnish with fresh parsley and serve right away.

Nutrition: Calories: 479; Fat: 17g; Carbs: 215.5g; Protein: 32.7g

Chopped Power Salad with Chicken

Preparation time: 20 minutes   Cooking time: 5 minutes

Ingredients:

- 4 boneless, skinless chicken breasts
- To taste: Salt and pepper
- 2 heads romaine lettuce, sliced
- 1-pint cherry tomatoes, divided
- 1 avocado, sliced
- 1/2 red onion, minced
- A half cup crumbled feta cheese
- 1/4 cup sliced fresh parsley
- 2 tbsp. of olive oil
- 2 tbsp. of red wine vinegar
- 1 clove garlic, sliced
- 1 tsp. of Dijon mustard
- Four boneless, skinless chicken breasts

Directions:

1. Add salt and pepper to the chicken for seasoning. Grill or pan-fry until it is fully cooked.

1. Mix the lettuce, tomatoes, avocado, red onion, feta cheese, and parsley together in a large bowl.

2. Mix the olive oil, red wine vinegar, garlic, and Dijon mustard in a small bowl with a whisk.

3. Combine the salad by adding the dressing and mixing it until it's thoroughly coated.

4. Chop the chicken and prepare it on top of the salad.

Nutrition: Calories: 340; Fat: 13g; Carbs: 43g; Protein: 15g

Honey Walnut Chicken

Preparation time: 5 minutes　　　　Cooking time: 30 minutes

Ingredients:

- 1 lb boneless, chicken breasts, sliced into bite-sized pieces
- 1/2 cup of cornstarch
- To taste: Salt and pepper
- 1/4 cup of vegetable oil
- 1/2 cup sliced walnuts
- 1/4 cup of honey

- 2 tbsp. soy sauce
- 1 tbsp. rice vinegar
- 1 tsp. sesame oil
- 1 tsp. sugar
- 1/4 tsp. of white pepper
- 1 tbsp. of cornstarch mixed with 1 tbsp. water (cornstarch slurry)

Directions:

1. Mix the corn flour, salt, and pepper in a small dish. To set the chicken pieces evenly, whisk them in the mixture.

2. In a sizable pan or wok, warm up the vegetable oil on medium-high heat.

3. Attach the chicken pieces and process for about 3 to 4 minutes each side, or until golden brown and done. After you set the chicken out of the pan, take it away.

4. In the same skillet, add the chopped walnuts and cook for 1-2 minutes. Remove the walnuts from the skillet and place them in a separate dish.

5. Take a small bowl and combine the honey, soy sauce, rice vinegar, sesame oil, sugar, and white pepper, mixing them together thoroughly.

6. Put the honey mixture in the same pan and bring it to a boil over medium-high heat.

7. Set in the corn flour slurry and keep stirring for about 1-2 minutes, or until the sauce has achieved a denser, more viscous consistency until the sauce thickens.

8. Attach the cooked chicken and toasted walnuts back into the pan and set to coat the chicken evenly with the sauce. Enjoy the chicken over steamed rice and garnish with additional sliced walnuts if desired.

Nutrition: Calories: 315; Fat: 9g; Carbs: 32g; Protein: 17g

Black Bean Risotto

Preparation time: 10 minutes   Cooking time: 35 minutes

Ingredients:

- 1 tbsp olive oil
- One small onion, diced
- Two cloves of garlic, minced
- 1 cup Arborio rice
- 3 cups vegetable broth
- One can of black beans, drained and rinsed
- 1/4 cup grated Parmesan cheese
- Salt and pepper, to taste
- Fresh cilantro for garnish

Directions:

1. Warm the olive oil in a sizable pan with a medium heat.
2. Also include simmer the garlic and onion until they are smooth.
3. The rice should be stirred for 2 minutes or until it becomes visible.
4. Gently attach the broth one ladle at a time, constantly tossing until the liquid is absorbed before attaching the next ladle.
5. Keep cooking and stirring the rice for about 18 to 20 minutes or until it is "al dente."
6. Add the black beans and Parmesan cheese and season the dish with salt and pepper to achieve the desired taste.
7. Cook until the cheese dissolves and the beans are heated through.
8. Add fresh cilantro as a garnish and serve right away.

Nutrition: Calories: 268; Fat: 8g; Carbs: 36g; Protein: 14g

Cilantro-Lime Chicken and Avocado Salsa

Preparation time: 10 minutes   Cooking time: 12 minutes

Ingredients:

- For the chicken
- 2 tablespoons minced fresh cilantro
- 11/2 tablespoons freshly squeezed lime juice
- 2 teaspoons olive oil
- 1/8 teaspoon salt
- 1/2 teaspoon ground cumin
- 2 (6-ounce) skinless, boneless chicken breasts
- Olive oil nonstick cooking spray
- For the salsa
- 1/2 cup chopped plum tomato
- 1/4 cup chopped red bell pepper

- 1 tablespoon finely chopped onion
- 2 tablespoons minced fresh cilantro
- 2 tablespoons freshly squeezed lime juice
- 1 small peach, peeled and finely chopped
- 1/8 teaspoon salt
- 1/8 teaspoon freshly ground black pepper
- 1/2 avocado, peeled and finely chopped

Directions:

To make the chicken

1. Put the cilantro, lime juice, cumin, salt, and olive oil in a medium dish. Chicken is added to the sauce and coated by tossing. Refrigerate for 30 minutes. Detach the chicken from the marinade and discard the marinade.
2. Fire a sizable grill pan or nonstick saucepan over high heat.
3. Sprat cooking spray on the pan. The chicken should be attached to the pan and grilled for 6 minutes on each side.

To set the salsa

1. In a medium bowl, combine the tomato, bell pepper, onion, cilantro, lime juice, peach salt and pepper. Add the avocado and stir gently to combine.
2. Serve the chicken topped with the salsa.

Nutrition: Calories: 366; Fat: 17g; Carbs: 15g; Protein: 41g

Green Beans and Mushrooms Spaghetti

Preparation time: 15 minutes

Cooking time: 15 minutes

Ingredients:

- 1 lb. spaghetti2 cloves of garlic, sliced
- 2 tbsp. of olive oil
- To taste: Salt and pepper

- 1 lb. green beans
- 8 oz. sliced mushrooms
- 1/4 cup grated Parmesan cheese
- 1/4 cup sliced fresh parsley

Directions:

1. Prepare the spaghetti according to the box instructions until it is al dente.
2. Strain, and then separate.
3. Heat a grill or grill pan over medium-high heat.
4. Set the green beans and mushrooms with garlic, olive oil, salt, and pepper.
5. Grill for 5-7 minutes or until crisp and slightly charred.
6. In a serving bowl, set the cooked spaghetti with the grilled green beans and mushrooms, grated Parmesan cheese, and sliced parsley.
7. Plate the dish and savor its flavors. Serve and enjoy.

Nutrition: Calories: 439; Fat: 9g; Carbs: 81g; Protein: 17g

Balsamic Rosemary Chicken

Preparation time: 10 minutes

Cooking time: 35 minutes

Ingredients:

- 1/2 cup balsamic vinegar, plus 2 tablespoons
- 1 teaspoon olive oil
- 1 tablespoon chopped fresh rosemary

- 1 garlic clove, minced
- 1/8 teaspoon salt
- Freshly ground black pepper
- Olive oil cooking spray

- 2 (6-ounce) boneless, skinless chicken breasts
- Fresh rosemary sprigs, for garnish

Directions:

1. Put together the rosemary, garlic, olive oil, salt, and pepper in a small pot along with 1/2 cup of balsamic vinegar.
2. Set the heat to medium-low, bring to a boil, and then stew for about 3 minutes, or until the liquid has been decreased by half.
3. Transfer the pan to the refrigerator for about 15 minutes or the freezer for about 5 minutes.
4. Cover a 9-by-9-inch baking dish with cooking spray.
5. Put the chicken into the baking dish and pour the marinade, which has been cooled, over the chicken.
6. Refrigerate for 30 minutes.
7. Set the oven to 400°F. Remove the dish from the refrigerator, cover it with aluminum foil and bake the chicken in the marinade for 35 minutes, or until an instant-read thermometer registers 165°F.
8. Transfer the chicken onto the serving plates. Transfer the cooked marinade into a small saucepan. Add the remaining 2 tablespoons of balsamic vinegar and cook for 5 minutes.
9. Arrange the sauce over the meat and top with fresh rosemary before serving.

Nutrition: Calories: 228; Fat: 4g; Carbs: 2g; Protein: 39

Turkey Sandwich

Preparation time: 5 minutes

Cooking time: 5 minutes

Ingredients:

- Two slices of bread (your choice)
- 2-3 slices of turkey deli meat
- 2-3 leaves of lettuce
- 2-3 slices of tomato
- 1-2 tbsp mayonnaise or mustard
- Salt and pepper, to taste

Directions:

1. If wanted, toast the bread slices.
2. Spread mayonnaise or mustard on one or both slices of bread.
3. Place the turkey deli meat on one slice of bread.
4. Add the lettuce, tomato, salt, and pepper to the turkey.
5. Secure the sandwich with the extra piece of bread.
6. If desired, divide the sandwich in 2.

Nutrition: Calories: 255; Fat: 11g; Carbs: 25g; Protein: 28g

Salmon and Summer Squash in Parchment

Preparation time: 15 minutes   Cooking time: 17 minutes

Ingredients:

- 2 tbsp. sliced shallot
- 1/8 tbsp, freshly ground black pepper
- 1 tbsp. chopped fresh oregano leaves
- 1/2 tbsp. olive oil
- 1/8 tbsp. salt

- 1 cup sliced yellow summer squash
- 1 cup sliced medium zucchini
- 2 skinless salmon fillets
- 2 tbsp. freshly squeezed lemon juice
- 1 tbsp. grated lemon zest, divided

Directions:

1. Turn the oven to 400°F.
2. In a medium bowl, combine the lemon juice, yellow squash, shallot, oregano, olive oil, salt, and pepper.
3. Place 2 large parchment rectangles on the work surface with the short side of the parchment closest to you. On 1/2 of one parchment rectangle, set half the zucchini slices lengthwise, overlapping them slightly. Place a salmon fillet on the zucchini, sprinkle with half the lemon zest, then top with half the yellow squash mixture. Fold the parchment over the ingredients. Repeat with the other piece of

parchment and the remaining ingredients. To seal the packets, begin at one corner and tightly fold over the edges about 1/2 inch all around, overlapping the folds.

4. Lay the packets on a baking sheet and process for about 17 minutes, or until the salmon turns opaque throughout.

5. To serve, carefully cut the packets open, being careful to avoid escaping steam, and with a spatula gently transfer the salmon and vegetables to two plates. Spoon any liquid remaining in the parchment over the salmon and vegetables.

Nutrition: Calories: 291; Fat: 15g; Carbs: 7g; Protein: 35g

Rainbow Trout Baked in Foil

Preparation time: 10 minutes   Cooking time: 15 minutes

Ingredients:

- Lemon wedges, for serving
- Freshly sliced parsley, for topping
- ½ tbsp. olive oil, divided, plus more for greasing the foil
- Freshly ground black pepper

- 1 cup peeled, seeded, and sliced tomato
- Freshly sliced thyme, for topping
- 4 fresh thyme sprigs
- 2 small rainbow trout, deboned
- 2 garlic cloves, minced
- Salt

Directions:

1. Preheat the oven to 450 degrees.
2. Two sheets of sturdy aluminum foil should be cut into rectangles that are three inches longer than your fish.
3. A trout should be placed skin-side down on each piece of foil after it has been greased with olive oil on the dull side.
4. Open them flat and season both sides with salt and pepper.
5. Add salt and pepper to a dish and combine the tomato, garlic, and 1 teaspoon of olive oil. Over each trout's center, place an equal quantity.

6. Fold the trout's two sides together, placing 2 thyme stems on top of each.

7. Over each fish, drizzle 1/4 teaspoon of olive oil.

8. Ensure that the trout are positioned in the center of each square before slipping the foil up loosely, grabbing it at the sides, and crimping it together firmly to form a packet. They should be baked for 10 to 15 minutes after being put on a baking tray.

9. The flesh should be opaque and easily rip apart when examined with a fork.

10. Put a plate with each package on it.

11. To open the packages, carefully cut across the top, being careful not to get burned by the steam. Pour the liquids over the fish after carefully removing it from the packets. Serve with lemon slices and a sprinkle of thyme and parsley.

Nutrition: Calories: 320; Fat: 16g; Carbs: 5g; Protein: 39g

Sesame-Crusted Tuna Steaks

Preparation time: 5 minutes

Cooking time: 12 minutes

Ingredients:

- Olive oil nonstick cooking spray
- 1/2 tablespoon olive oil
- 1 teaspoon sesame oil
- 2 (6-ounce) ahi tuna steaks
- 6 tablespoons sesame seeds
- Salt
- Freshly ground black pepper

Directions:

1. Lightly spray a baking sheet with cooking oil and preheat the oven to 450°F.

2. Mix the sesame oil and olive oil in a small dish.

3. Apply the oil mixture to the tuna fillets in a brush.

4. Fill a small dish with sesame seeds.

5. Press the steaks into the seeds, turning to cover all sides.

6. Set the prepped baking sheet with the tuna steaks on it.

7. Add salt and pepper.

8. Fish should be baked for 4 to 6 minutes per half-inch of width, or until a fork inserted into the center of the fish begins to flake.

9. Serve immediately.

Nutrition: Calories: 520; Fat: 30g; Carbs: 6g; Protein: 56g

Salmon and Scallop Skewers

Preparation time: 30 minutes

Cooking time: 12 minutes

Ingredients:

- 1 (8-ounce) can pineapple chunks in 100% pineapple juice, drained, reserving 2 tablespoons juice
- 1 tablespoon freshly squeezed lemon juice
- 1 tablespoon snipped fresh tarragon or 1 teaspoon dried tarragon
- 1/4 teaspoon dry mustard
- 1/8 teaspoon salt

- 4 ounces skinless, boneless wild salmon fillets, cut into 1-inch cubes
- 4 ounces scallops
- 1 zucchini, cut into 1/2-inch-thick slices
- 1 red bell pepper, sliced into 1-inch squares
- 1 red onion, cut into 1-inch pieces
- 8 button mushrooms

Directions:

1. Preheat an outdoor grill. In a small bowl, combine the 2 tablespoons of reserved pineapple juice, the lemon juice, tarragon, mustard, and salt.

2. Place the salmon and scallops in a resealable bag, add the marinade and seal the bag.

3. Turn the fish and scallops to coat well. Set and marinate in the refrigerator for 1 to 2 hours, turning once.

4. In a small saucepan, bring just enough water to cover the zucchini (1 to 2 inches) to a boil.

5. Set the zucchini and cook, sealed, for 3 to 4 minutes, or until nearly tender. Drain and cool.

6. Remove the seafood from the bag, reserving the marinade.

7. On 4 metal skewers, alternately thread the scallops salmon, zucchini, mushrooms, bell pepper, onion, and pineapple.

8. Coat with the marinade set aside earlier by using a brush.

9. Grill, uncovered, directly over medium coals for 8 to 12 minutes, turning once, until the scallops turn opaque and the salmon flakes easily when tested with a fork.

10. Serve two skewers on each dinner plate.

Nutrition: Calories: 260; Fat: 5g; Carbs: 32g; Protein: 26g

Shrimp Scampi with Zoodles

Preparation time: 10 minutes   Cooking time: 30 minutes

Ingredients:

- 1 pound of raw shrimp, peeled and deveined
- 4 cloves of garlic, minced
- 1/4 cup of butter
- 1/4 cup of olive oil
- 1/4 cup of fresh lemon juice
- 2 tablespoons of chopped parsley
- Salt and pepper, to taste
- 2 medium-sized zucchini, spiralized into "zoodles"

Directions:

1. In a big pan, cook the butter and olive oil over medium-high heat.
2. When the garlic has a nice smokiness, add it and cook it for 1-2 minutes.
3. Season the prawns with salt and pepper after placing them in the pan.
4. Cook for about 3–5 minutes, or until the shrimp are pink and cooked all the way through.
5. Take the shrimp out of the pan and put them on a plate.
6. Add the lemon juice to the pan and stir it to get any browned bits off the bottom. Process for another 1-2 minutes.

7. Put the zoodles in the pan and toss them with the sauce to coat them. Cook the zoodles for 2 to 3 minutes, until they are soft but still firm.

8. Set the shrimp back in the pan and whisk everything together.

9. Serve the scampi on top of the zoodles and add chopped parsley on top.

Nutrition: Calories: 286; Fat: 15g; Carbs: 8g; Protein: 27g

Lemon Garlic Mackerel

Preparation time: 10 minutes   Cooking time: 5 minutes

Ingredients:

- 2 (4-ounce) mackerel fillets
- Salt
- 2 garlic cloves, minced
- Juice of 1/2 lemon
- Freshly ground black pepper

Directions:

1. Prepare a baking sheet with aluminum foil and set the fillets on it. Sprinkle them with salt and leave them for 5 minutes. This helps give the fish a firmer texture.

2. In a bowl, set together the garlic, lemon juice, and some pepper.

3. Evenly distribute the mixture over the mackerel.

4. Broil for about 5 minutes. Serve immediately.

Nutrition: Calories: 302; Fat: 20g; Carbs: 1g; Protein: 27g

Broiled Tuna Steaks with Lime

Preparation time: 5 minutes   Cooking time: 8 minutes

Ingredients:

- Olive oil nonstick cooking spray
- 2 (6-ounce) tuna steaks
- 1 teaspoon freshly grated lime zest
- 1/8 teaspoon salt

- 1/2 teaspoon freshly ground black pepper
- 1 garlic clove, minced
- Lemon wedges, for serving

Directions:

1. Preheat the broiler and apply cooking spray to the broiler.
2. Place the fish in the prepared broiler pan.
3. In a dish, merge the lime zest, salt, pepper, and garlic. Set together the mixture over the fish.
4. Broil for 7 to 8 minutes, or until the fish is cooked to your preference or flakes readily when tested with a fork.
5. Transfer each steak to a serving plate and serve with lemon wedges.

Nutrition: Calories: 317; Fat: 11g; Carbs: 1g; Protein: 51g

Oven-Roasted Salmon Fillets

Preparation time: 5 minutes   Cooking time: 15 minutes

Ingredients:

- 1 (6-ounce) salmon fillet, divided into 2 pieces
- Salt
- Freshly ground black pepper
- 1 lemon, cut into wedges, for garnish
- Parsley, for garnish

Directions:

1. Turn the oven to 450°F.
2. Apply a small amount of salt and black pepper to the salmon.
3. Place the salmon on a nonstick baking sheet or in a nonstick pan with an ovenproof handle, ensuring that the skin side is facing downwards.
4. Process until is cooked through and flakes easily with a fork 12 to 15 minutes.
5. Serve with the lemon wedges and fresh parsley.

Nutrition: Calories: 113; Fat: 5g; Carbs: 0g; Protein: 17

Moroccan Spiced Chicken with Onions

Preparation time: 15 minutes   Cooking time: 20 minutes

Ingredients:

- 1 teaspoon ground cinnamon
- 1 teaspoon paprika
- 3/4 teaspoon ground cumin
- 1/2 teaspoon ground cardamom
- 1/2 teaspoon ground coriander
- 1/2 teaspoon ground ginger
- 1/2 teaspoon ground turmeric

- 1 tablespoon olive oil, divided
- 2 (6-ounce) skinless, boneless chicken breasts
- 1/8 teaspoon salt
- Olive oil nonstick cooking spray
- 1 cup sliced yellow onion
- 1 teaspoon honey

Directions:

1. Mix up the turmeric, ginger, coriander, cumin, paprika, and cardamom in a small dish.

2. In a sizable ovenproof skillet over medium-low heat, soften 1/2 spoonful of the olive oil, stirring to coat the pan. Stirring regularly, add the spice mixture to the skillet and cook for three minutes, or until the spices are toasted. Chicken breasts should be placed in a sizable resealable bag along with the spice combination, sealed, and given a goof shake to coat. Chicken is seasoned, then put in the fridge for then minutes.

3. Set the oven's temperature to 350°F.

4. Take out the chicken from the bag and evenly sprinkle some salt on it. Cooking spray is gently applied to the skillet before heating it up over medium-high heat. Cook for about 4 minutes with the poultry attached. Cook for an additional minute after flipping the poultry. Take the poultry out of the pan.

5. Swirl in the remaining 1/2 spoonful of olive oil to coat the pan. The onion should be added and sautéed for 2 minutes, or until it begins to color. Put the honey into the pan and add the poultry back. Bake for 10 minutes, or until an instant-read thermometer registers 165°F. Serve immediately.

Nutrition: Calories: 295; Fat: 10g; Carbs: 11g; Protein: 40g

Spaghetti Squash and Chickpea Sauté

Preparation time: 5 minutes

Cooking time: 15 minutes

Ingredients:

- 1 medium spaghetti squash, halved and seeded
- 2 tbsp olive oil
- 1 onion, diced
- 2 cloves of garlic, minced
- 1 can (15 oz) chickpeas, drained and rinsed
- 1/2 cup vegetable broth
- 1/4 cup diced tomatoes
- 1 tsp dried oregano
- 1 tsp dried basil
- 1/4 tsp red pepper flakes (optional)
- Salt and pepper, to taste
- 1/4 cup chopped fresh parsley or cilantro (optional)
- Grated Parmesan cheese, for serving (optional)

Directions:

1. Adjust the oven to a temperature of 375°F. Set the cut-side-down spaghetti squash halves on a baking sheet sealed with parchment paper. Roast for 30 to 40 minutes, or until the flesh is soft and the threads readily break apart with a fork.

2. Set out of the oven, then allow to cool for a while. Use a fork to scrape the spaghetti-like strands out of the skin once it is cool enough to handle, then set them aside. Olive oil should be heated in a sizable skillet over medium heat. Garlic and onion should be attached and sautéed for 2-3 minutes, or until crisp.

3. Attach the sliced tomatoes, oregano, red pepper flakes, basil, salt, and pepper to the chickpeas, vegetable broth, and other ingredients.

4. For 5-7 minutes, or until the sauce has slightly thickened, bring to a simmer. Stir in the spaghetti squash strands and process for an additional 2-3 minutes or until heated through.

5. Remove from heat and stir in fresh parsley or cilantro (if using).

6. Serve with grated Parmesan cheese on top, if desired.

Nutrition: Calories: 245; Fat: 10g; Carbs: 27g; Protein: 7g

Grilled Chicken Breasts with Plum Salsa

Preparation time: 5 minutes   Cooking time: 12 minutes

Ingredients:

For the chicken

- 1/8 tbsp. salt
- 1 tbsp. olive oil
- 1/4 tbsp. ground cumin
- ¼ tbsp. garlic powder

- 2 skinless, boneless chicken breasts
- 1 tbsp. brown sugar

For the plum salsa

- 2 tbsp. chopped red bell pepper
- 1/4 tbsp. hot sauce
- 2 tbsp. sliced red onion

- 1/8 tbsp. salt
- 1 cup sliced ripe plum
- 2 tbsp. cider vinegar

Directions:

1. Put together the brown sugar, cumin, garlic powder, and salt in a small dish.
2. Apply the mixture all over the poultry.
3. In a nonstick skillet or griddle pan, warm the olive oil over medium heat.
4. The chicken should be connected and cooked for 6 minutes on each side.
5. 1 an instant-read thermometer reads 165°F.

Nutrition: Calories: 265; Fat: 5g; Carbs: 16g; Protein: 41g

Pesto Pasta

Preparation time: 5 minutes   Cooking time: 10 minutes

Ingredients:

- 2 cups of fresh basil leaves
- 1/2 cup of extra-virgin olive oil

- To taste: Salt and pepper,

- 1/2 cup of grated Parmesan cheese
- 1/2 cup of pine nuts
- 3 cloves of garlic
- 1 lb. of pasta of your choice

Directions:

1. In a food processor, merge the basil leaves, Parmesan cheese, pine nuts, and garlic.
2. Pulse until finely minced.
3. Slowly spill the olive oil through the feed tube with the food processor running.
4. Flavor with salt and pepper to taste.
5. Cook the pasta as instructed on the package and retain 1 cup of the pasta cooking water.
6. Pasta should be drained before being combined with pesto in a food processor.
7. Once everything is thoroughly blended, pulse.
8. If more pasta water is needed to achieve the appropriate consistency, add it.
9. Serve immediately and garnish with additional Parmesan cheese and pine nuts.

Nutrition: Calories: 225; Fat: 7g; Carbs: 32g; Protein: 8g

Chicken Kebabs Mexicana

Preparation time: 30 minutes

Cooking time: 10 minutes

Ingredients:

- 1 pound boneless, skinless chicken breast, cut into 1-inch cubes
- 1/4 cup olive oil
- 2 cloves of garlic, minced
- 1 teaspoon ground cumin
- 1 teaspoon smoked paprika
- 1 teaspoon dried oregano
- 1/2 teaspoon salt
- 1/4 teaspoon black pepper
- 1 red bell pepper, cut into 1-inch cubes
- 1 onion, cut into wedges
- 12 skewers

Directions:

1. In a mixing bowl, merge the olive oil, oregano, cumin, garlic, paprika, salt, and pepper.

2. Put the chicken cubes in the bowl and toss them around so the marinade covers them evenly. For best results, cover and put in the fridge for at least an hour or overnight.

3. Set your grill or broiler to medium-high heat.

4. Alternate the chicken cubes, bell pepper, and onion as you thread them onto the skewers.

5. Grill or broil the kebabs for about 8 to 10 minutes per side, or until the chicken is fully cooked and the vegetables are slightly charred.

6. You can top the chicken kebabs with sour cream, avocado, cilantro, or anything else you like.

Nutrition: Calories: 166; Fat: 8g; Carbs: 9g; Protein: 15g

Chicken Cutlets with Pineapple Rice

Preparation time: 10 minutes   Cooking time: 20 minutes

Ingredients:

- Four boneless, skinless chicken cutlets
- Salt and pepper, to taste
- 1/2 cup all-purpose flour
- Two eggs, beaten
- 1 cup panko breadcrumbs

- 1 cup diced pineapple
- 1 cup uncooked white rice
- 2 cups chicken broth
- One tablespoon vegetable oil
- One teaspoon soy sauce

Directions:

1. Set the oven to 375°F (190°C). Salt and pepper the chicken cutlets, then coat them in flour and shake off any extra.

2. The cutlets are coated in panko breadcrumbs after being dipped in beaten eggs.

3. Put the oil in a large pan and heat it over medium-high heat.

4. When the pan is warm, attach the chicken cutlets and cook for 2 to 3 minutes each side, or until golden brown.

5. In a warmth oven, set the chicken cutlets in a baking tray and process them for 10-12 minutes.

6. In a saucepan, take the chicken broth to a boil. In a pan, merge together the rice, pineapple, and soy sauce.

7. Set the heat down to low, seal, and let it boil for 18-20 minutes, or until the rice is soft and all the liquid has been consumed.

Nutrition: Calories: 529; Fat: 9g; Carbs: 72g; Protein: 37g

DINNER RECIPES

Oven-Roasted Salmon with Vinaigrette

Preparation time: 5 minutes   Cooking time: 24-25 minutes

Ingredients:

- 3 6-oz. salmon fillets
- To taste: Salt and pepper
- 2 lemons divided
- 2 tbsp. of olive oil
- 1/4 cup sliced fresh parsley

Directions:

1. Set your oven to 425°F (220°C) and turn it on.
2. Attach salt and pepper to the salmon fillets.
3. Slice side down, set the lemon halves on a baking sheet. Put the salmon fillets and lemon halves on the baking sheet.
4. Olive oil should be poured over the salmon and lemons.
5. Roast the salmon in an oven that has already been heated for 12 to 15 minutes, or until it is done the way you like it.
6. While the salmon is roasting, make the vinaigrette by squeezing the juice from the roasted lemon halves into a small bowl. Mix in chopped parsley.
7. Once the salmon is finished roasting, remove it from the oven. Drizzle the charred lemon vinaigrette over the salmon and serve immediately.

Nutrition: Calories: 322; Fat: 18g; Carbs: 10g; Protein: 32g

Portobello Mushrooms with Mozzarella

Preparation time: 10 minutes   Cooking time: 50 minutes

Ingredients:

- 1/2 tablespoon olive oil
- 11/2 cups diced onion
- Salt
- Freshly ground black pepper
- 2 portobello mushrooms,
- 6 tablespoons shredded part-skim mozzarella cheese
- 1 cup sliced zucchini

Directions:

1. Turn the oven to 350°F and set a baking pan with parchment paper.
2. Place a medium-sized saucepan on the stovetop and heat the olive oil gradually over medium heat.
3. Add the onion and cook for about 20 minutes, or until soft and browned. If the onions begin to stick, attach a little water and cook until the water evaporates. Season with salt and pepper.
4. Place the mushrooms in the baking pan, stemmed-side up. Pack half of the cooked onions and half of the mozzarella in each mushroom cap.
5. Lay the sliced zucchini beside the mushrooms in the baking pan. Set with salt and pepper. Bake for 30 minutes and serve warm.

Nutrition: Calories: 171; Fat: 8g; Carbs: 19g; Protein: 10g

Chicken Kebabs

Preparation time: 15 minutes   Cooking time: 45 minutes

Ingredients:

- 1 pound boneless, skinless chicken breasts cut into 1-inch cubes
- One red bell pepper, cut into 1-inch squares
- One yellow onion, cut into 1-inch squares
- 1/4 cup olive oil

- Two cloves of garlic, minced
- Two tablespoons of lemon juice
- Two teaspoons of ground cumin
- One teaspoon of ground paprika
- Salt and pepper, to taste
- Skewers (if using wooden skewers, soak them in water for at least 30 minutes before using

Directions:

1. Mix the olive oil, garlic, lemon juice, cumin, salt, paprika, and pepper together in a large bowl.

2. Attach the chicken, bell pepper, and onion to the dish. Toss everything together until the marinade covers everything well. Set the bowl in the fridge for at least 30 minutes and up to 2 hours, sealed with plastic wrap.

3. Set your grill's heat to medium-high.

4. Alternately thread the chicken, bell pepper, and onion onto skewers.

5. Roast the kebabs for 8-10 minutes, turning them often until the chicken is fully processed and the vegetables have a little char.

6. Serve right away with the side dish of your choice.

Note: If you don't have a grill, cook the kebabs in a grill pan or broil them in the oven.

Nutrition: Calories: 220; Fat: 2.2g; Carbs: 35g; Protein: 15g

Indian Spiced Cauliflower Fried Rice

Preparation time: 10 minutes   Cooking time: 10 minutes

Ingredients:

- 2 teaspoons olive oil, divided
- 2 eggs, beaten
- 2 garlic cloves, finely minced
- 1/4 cup finely sliced red bell pepper
- 1/4 cup finely sliced carrots
- 1/4 cup finely chopped onion
- 3 cups grated cauliflower
- 1 cup frozen shelled edamame
- 1/2 teaspoon ground cumin
- 1/4 teaspoon ground ginger
- 1/8 teaspoon ground cardamom
- 1/8 teaspoon ground cinnamon
- Freshly ground black pepper
- 1 cup finely chopped fresh spinach
- 2 teaspoons Bragg's liquid aminos (or low-sodium soy sauce)
- 1/4 cup cashews, for garnish

Directions:

1. Heat 1 tbsp. of olive oil in a large sauté pan. Attach the eggs and slowly stir until curds form, then fold the curds over themselves until there is no more liquid egg. Bring from the heat and break into small pieces. Bring the eggs to a plate.

2. Warm up the final spoonful of olive oil. Sauté the garlic for 30 seconds after attaching. For two minutes, add the bell pepper, carrots, and onion. Cook, stirring, for 5 to 8 minutes after adding the broccoli, edamame, cumin, ginger, cardamom, cinnamon, and a few grinds of pepper. Add the greens and cook for 2 minutes, or until wilted.

3. Set the Bragg's aminos and the cooked egg and stir well to combine. Remove from the heat and divide equally between two bowls. Sprinkle with the cashews and serve.

Nutrition: Calories: 386; Fat: 22g; Carbs: 29g; Protein: 27g

Tofu Vegetable Stir-Fry

Preparation time: 15 minutes   Cooking time: 35 minutes

Ingredients:

For the sauce

- 1 tbsp. rice wine vinegar
- 3 to 4 tbsp. water
- 1 tbsp. cornstarch

- 1 tbsp. peeled and grated fresh ginger
- 2 tbsp. low-sodium soy sauce
- 1 tbsp. honey

For the stir-fry

- 1 tbsp. olive oil
- 1 package firm or extra-firm tofu, drained for 15 minutes

- 1 cup snow peas 1 cup sliced red bell pepper
- 1 cup broccoli florets

Directions:

1. In a mixing bowl, set together all the sauce ingredients and set it aside.
1. Set a baking pan in the oven and preheat it to 400 degrees Fahrenheit.
2. Arrange the tofu pieces on the baking sheet that has been prepared. To guarantee even cooking, bake for 25 to 35 minutes, flipping halfway through. When the tofu

is slightly firm and golden brown, take it out of the oven and let it cool while you prepare the veggies.

3. In a big pan over medium-high heat, warm the olive oil. Cook the bell pepper, broccoli, and snow peas for 5 to 7 minutes while frequently turning. Once the veggies have begun to soften and take on some color, attach the sauce to the pan and stir. It ought to thicken and froth.

4. Add the tofu and give it a good mix. Stirring frequently, cook the combination for 3 to 5 minutes. Remove from the fire and serve the vegetables once they are cooked to your preference.

Nutrition: Calories: 331; Fat: 16g; Carbs: 31g; Protein: 21g

Pocket Eggs with Sesame Sauce

Preparation time: 5 minutes   Cooking time: 5 minutes

Ingredients:

- 1/4 tbsp. freshly ground black pepper
- 1/2 tbsp. rice vinegar
- 2 tbsp. low-sodium soy sauce
- 4 large eggs
- 1 tbsp sesame oil

- 1 tbsp. minced scallions
- 2 tbsp. olive oil
- 1 tbsp. black or white sesame seeds
- 1 tbsp. dried basil

Directions:

1. Combine the soy sauce, sesame oil, vinegar, and scallions in a small dish. Leave it alone.
2. In a medium nonstick pan over medium heat, warm the olive oil and stir to coat. Crack the remaining 2 eggs into a second tiny bowl after cracking the first two into it.
3. Quickly pour two eggs on one side of the pan and the remaining two on the other side. The egg whites will blend into one big chunk as they flow together.
4. Top the eggs with the sesame seeds, cilantro, and pepper. Cook for about 3 minutes, or until the yolks are completely set and the egg whites are crunchy and

golden brown on the bottom. Using a broad spatula to flip the eggs without breaking them, cook them for an additional 1 to 2 minutes, or until the whites are crispy and golden brown on the other side.

5. Cover the eggs with the marinade you saved. Stir the eggs once to ensure that the marinade in on both sides and simmer for 30 seconds. Slice into slices and top with pan sauce before serving.

Nutrition: Calories: 241; Fat: 19g; Carbs: 3g; Protein: 14g

Lentil Walnut Burgers

Preparation time: 10 minutes   Cooking time: 10 minutes

Ingredients:

- 1/2 cup chopped red onion
- 1/3 cup walnuts
- 1/4 cup packed fresh cilantro leaves
- 1 garlic clove, minced
- 1/4-inch piece fresh ginger, peeled
- 3/4 teaspoon ground coriander
- 3/4 teaspoon ground cumin
- 1/2 teaspoon paprika

- 1/8 teaspoon salt
- 3/4 cup cooked brown rice
- 1 (15-ounce) can lentils, drained and rinsed, divided
- 1 egg, beaten
- 1 teaspoon olive oil, plus a drizzle
- 3 tablespoons gluten-free oat flour
- 1 cup chopped romaine leaves

Directions:

1. Place the onion, walnuts, cilantro, garlic, and ginger in a food processor and pulse until thoroughly chopped. Add the coriander, cumin, paprika, salt, rice, and half the lentils and pulse a few times until well combined. Transfer to a bowl and add the remaining lentils. Mix in the egg and oil after adding them. Mix in the wheat flour after adding it.
2. Chill in the refrigerator for 10 minutes.
3. Form the mixture into 4 burgers that are tightly compressed. Add some olive oil to a big pan and heat it up on medium-high. The patties should be cooked for 4 to 6 minutes on each side in the pan.

4. Divide the romaine leaves equally between two serving plates. Top reach pile of romaine with 2 burgers and serve warm.

Nutrition: Calories: 241; Fat: 19g; Carbs: 3g; Protein: 14g

Zucchini "Spaghetti" with Almond Pesto

Preparation time: 10 minutes   Cooking time: 10 minutes

Ingredients:

- 1 cup loosely packed fresh basil leaves
- 1/3 cup roasted, unsalted almonds
- 1/2 tablespoon sherry vinegar
- 1/8 teaspoon salt
- 1 teaspoon olive oil

- 2 garlic cloves, minced
- 1/2 red onion, sliced
- 1 cup green peas (fresh or frozen and thawed)
- 2 medium zucchini, julienned or cut into long noodles with spiralizer or vegetable peeler

Directions:

1. To a food blender, add the almonds, vinegar, salt, and 1/2 cup of basil.
2. As you pulse, frequently scrape down the food processor's edges to create a smooth paste.
3. Scrape into a dish, then reserve.
4. Use a medium-sized pan on medium heat to warm the olive oil.
5. Sauté for 2 to 4 minutes, or until the onion is translucent and the peas are fully done, after adding the garlic, onion, and beans.
6. Attach the zucchini noodles to the skillet and cook for 1 to 2 minutes.
7. Stir in the mixture often.
8. Add the pesto to the skillet, toss to merge, and cook for 1 to 2 minutes, or just enough to warm through.
9. Remove from the heat and divide between two plates, top with the remaining half cup of basil leaves, and serve.

Nutrition: Calories: 220; Fat: 11g; Carbs: 24g; Protein: 11g

Farro with Sun-Dried Tomatoes

Preparation time: 5 minutes   Cooking time: 40 minutes

Ingredients:

- 1/2 tablespoon olive oil
- 1 large shallot, diced
- 1/4 cup julienned water-packed sun-dried tomatoes, drained
- 4 ounces uncooked farro
- 1 cup low-sodium vegetable broth
- 2 to 3 cups loosely packed arugula
- 4 or 5 large fresh basil leaves, thinly sliced
- 1/4 cup pine nuts

Directions:

1. Prepare a large pan over medium-high heat and incorporate the olive oil. Add the onion and sauté until golden, about 5 minutes.
2. Add the sun-dried tomatoes and farro to the skillet and sauté for about 30 seconds to toast the farro.
3. Add the vegetable broth, stir to merge, and set together the mixture to a boil. Set the heat to low, cover, and simmer for 30 minutes, or until the farro is tender.
4. Stir in the arugula and basil and cook for 1 to 2 minutes, or until wilted. Add the pine nuts and toss to combine. Serve warm.

Nutrition: Calories: 350; Fat: 17g; Carbs: 39g; Protein: 13g

One-Skillet Quinoa and Vegetables

Preparation time: 10 minutes   Cooking time: 30 minutes

Ingredients:

- 1/2 tablespoon olive oil
- 1/2 cup chopped sweet onion
- 1/4 cup chopped red bell pepper
- 1 cup chopped tomato, with juices
- 1/2 cup quinoa, rinsed
- 1/2 cup water

- 1/2 cup corn kernels
- 1 can black beans, drained and rinsed
- 1/2 teaspoon chili powder
- 1/2 teaspoon ground cumin
- Salt
- Freshly ground black pepper

- 1/4 cup chopped fresh cilantro, for garnish (optional)
- Avocado slices, for garnish (optional)
- 1 lime, sliced, for garnish (optional)

Directions:

1. In a skillet, set the olive oil over medium heat.
2. Sauté the onion and bell pepper for 3 to 4 minutes, or until softened.
3. Include the tomato and any juices with the quinoa, water, maize, black beans, cumin, chili powder, and salt and pepper to taste. The quinoa concoction should come to a boil.
4. Reduce the heat, cover the pan, and boil for 20 to 25 minutes, or until the liquid has completely evaporated.
5. Take the dish off the heat and split it between two plates.
6. Serve warm and garnish with the cilantro, avocado pieces, and fresh lime (if using).

Nutrition: Calories: 533; Fat: 11g; Carbs: 24g; Protein: 11g

Tarragon Sweet Potato and Egg Skillet

Preparation time: 5 minutes

Cooking time: 20 minutes

Ingredients:

- 2 large eggs
- 1 tbsp. dried tarragon
- 1/8 tbsp. salt
- 1/8 tbsp. freshly ground black pepper
- 2 medium sweet potatoes, cut into 1/2-inch chunks

- 1/4 cup nutritional yeast or low-fat cheese
- 1/2 cup water
- 1/2 cup sliced tomato
- 1/2 tbsp. olive oil
- 1/4 cup thinly sliced scallions

Directions:

1. Warm the olive oil in a sizable pan with a medium heat. Add the sweet potatoes and sprinkle with the tarragon, salt, and pepper. Stir, seal, and cook for about 5 minutes, stirring halfway through.

2. Stir in the water and tomato, cover again, and cook for about 10 more minutes, or until the potatoes are tender, stirring occasionally. If the skillet starts to get too dry, add a bit more water, 1 to 2 tablespoons at a time.

3. When the potatoes are tender, sprinkle the nutritional yeast evenly over the top.

4. Make two small wells in the sweet potatoes, leaving a few sweet potatoes at the bottom of each well.

5. Add one egg into each individual well and the whites are cooked to your preference, after sealing the skillet and lowering the heat to medium-low or low.

6. Detach from the heat and sprinkle with the scallions.

7. Serve warm.

Nutrition: Calories: 437; Fat: 11g; Carbs: 66g; Protein: 14g

Black-Eyed Pea Collard Wraps with Sauce

Preparation time: 10 minutes   Cooking time: 10 minutes

Ingredients:

For the sauce

- 1/3 cup unsalted natural peanut butter
- 2 tablespoons rice vinegar
- 1 teaspoon honey
- 1 tablespoon peeled and grated ginger
- 2 tablespoons water
- Dash sriracha
- Salt

For the wraps

- 6 large collard leaves, washed and dried
- 1/3 cup grated carrots
- 1 cucumber, peeled and julienned
- 1 can black-eyed peas, drained and rinsed

Directions:

To make the sauce

1. In a small bowl, set together all the ingredients for the sauce, making sure to eliminate any lumps in the peanut butter.

To make the wraps

1. Trim the center stem of each collard leaf lengthwise so it is more flexible.
2. Spread a spoonful of the peanut sauce on the inner side of each leaf, then layer a sixth of the carrots, cucumber, and black-eyed peas on each leaf.
3. To wrap, fold in the sides of the leaf and roll it up as you would a burrito.
4. Secure each wrap with a toothpick.
5. Arrange three wraps on each plate and serve.

Nutrition: Calories: 343; Fat: 22g; Carbs: 26g; Protein: 14g

Braised Cauliflower and Squash Penne

Preparation time: 10 minutes   Cooking time: 20 minutes

Ingredients:

- 11/2 teaspoons olive oil
- 2 garlic cloves, minced
- 1 teaspoon dried thyme
- 1/8 teaspoon red pepper flakes
- 1 cup low-sodium vegetable broth
- 1 cup unsweetened almond milk
- 4 ounces whole-wheat penne
- 1 cup (1-inch pieces) cauliflower florets
- 1 cup (1-inch cubes) peeled butternut squash
- 1 cup fresh butter beans, or canned, drained and rinsed
- Freshly ground black pepper

Directions:

1. Heat the olive oil in a saucepan of medium size over medium-high heat.
2. By stirring constantly, add the garlic, rosemary, and red pepper flakes.
3. Cook for one minute.
4. Add the broth, almond milk, penne, cauliflower, squash, and beans.

5. Bring to a boil, decrease the heat, and cook at a lively simmer, uncovered, for 10 to 15 minutes, or until the pasta is tender and the liquid has thickened and is greatly reduced.

6. Remove from the heat, stir in some pepper, and let it stand for 5 minutes.

7. Serve warm.

Nutrition: Calories: 447; Fat: 6g; Carbs: 79g; Protein: 19g

Mushroom Frittata

Preparation time: 10 minutes   Cooking time: 20 minutes

Ingredients:

- 4 eggs, slightly beaten
- 1 tablespoon chopped fresh basil
- 1/8 teaspoon salt
- 1/4 teaspoon freshly ground black pepper
- 1 tablespoon olive oil
- 2 cups chopped shiitake mushrooms

- 1/3 cup chopped scallions
- 1/4 cup shredded low-fat Cheddar cheese
- Sprigs of fresh thyme, for garnish
- Basil leaves, for garnish

Directions:

1. Whisk together the eggs, basil, salt, and pepper in a medium dish. Leave it alone.
2. In a tiny nonstick pan, prepare the olive oil.
3. Add the onions and mushrooms.
4. Cook the mushrooms for an approximately 5 minutes, stirring periodically, or until they are soft.
5. Preheat the broiler.
6. Set the egg mixture over the vegetables in the skillet.
7. Cook over medium heat and as the egg mixture sets, set a spatula around the sides so that uncooked egg can slide underneath.
8. Continue until the egg mixture is almost set, about 10 minutes; the surface should be just a little moist.

9. Sprinkle the cheese over the top.

10. Place the skillet 4 to 5 inches from the heat source and broil for 1 to 2 minutes, or until the top is set and the cheese has melted.

11. Serve topped with sprigs of thyme and basil.

Nutrition: Calories: 330; Fat: 19g; Carbs: 23g; Protein: 19g

Egg, Carrot, and Kale Salad Bowl

Preparation time: 10 minutes   Cooking time: 20 minutes

Ingredients:

- 1/2 cup uncooked quinoa, rinsed
- 1 cup water
- 1 cup sliced carrots
- 4 radishes, sliced
- 1/2 fennel bulb, sliced very finely
- 1 medium avocado, pitted, peeled, and cubed
- 2 cups stemmed and chopped baby kale
- 2 cups mixed baby lettuce
- 3 teaspoons olive oil, divided
- 2 teaspoons freshly squeezed lemon juice
- Pinch salt
- Pinch freshly ground black pepper
- 2 tablespoons tahini (sesame paste)
- 2 eggs
- 2 teaspoons hemp seeds

Directions:

1. Add the quinoa and water to a medium saucepan.

2. Set to a boil, lower the heat to a parboil, and process for about 15 minutes, or until tender.

3. Transfer to a large mixing bowl and set it aside to cool.

4. Add the carrots, radishes, fennel, avocado, kale, and lettuce to the quinoa.

5. Drizzle with 2 tablespoons of olive oil, the lemon juice, salt, and pepper and toss to merge.

6. Divide the salad between two bowls and drizzle 1 tablespoon of tahini over the salad in each bowl.

7. Heat the remaining 1 teaspoon of olive oil in a nonstick skillet over medium heat. Crack the eggs into the skillet, increase the heat to medium-high, and fry the eggs until cooked to your liking, about 3 minutes for over-hard.

8. Transfer one egg to each bowl, top each with 1 teaspoon of hemp seed, and serve immediately.

Nutrition: Calories: 660; Fat: 7g; Carbs: 46g; Protein: 22g

Grilled Squash Garlic Bread

Preparation time: 15 minutes   Cooking time: 15 minutes

Ingredients:

- One medium-sized yellow squash, sliced
- One medium-sized zucchini, sliced
- Two cloves of garlic, minced
- 1 tbsp olive oil
- Salt and pepper, to taste
- One loaf of French bread

Directions:

1. Preheat the grill to medium-high heat.
2. In a bowl, merge the sliced squash and zucchini with minced garlic, salt, olive oil, and pepper. Toss to coat.
3. Put the vegetables on the grill and process them for about 8- 10 minutes, or until they are soft and have a little bit of a char.
4. While the vegetables are cooking on the grill, cut the French bread into slices that are 1 inch thick. Set the olive oil on the slices and flavor them with salt and pepper.
5. Once the vegetables are done, remove them from the grill and place the bread slices on the grill. Roast for about 2-3 minutes per side or until toasted.
6. Once the bread is toasted, please remove it from the grill and top it with the grilled vegetables. Serve immediately.

Nutrition: Calories: 325; Fat: 14g; Carbs: 29g; Protein: 12g

Turkish-Style Minted Chickpea Salad

Preparation time: 10 minutes

Cooking time: 0 minutes

Ingredients:

- 1/2 cup roughly chopped fresh flat-leaf parsley
- 1/2 cup roughly chopped fresh mint leaves
- 1/2 cup drained and chopped oil-packed sun-dried tomatoes
- 1 (7.5-ounce) jar water-packed artichoke hearts, drained, rinsed, and chopped
- 1/4 cup pitted and chopped
- Kalamata olives

- 1/4 cup finely chopped red onion
- 11/2 tablespoons tomato sauce, no salt added
- 1 tablespoon freshly squeezed lemon juice
- 1/2 tablespoon olive oil
- 1/2 teaspoon paprika
- 1 (15-ounce) can chickpeas, drained and rinsed
- 1/2 cup finely chopped seedless cucumber

Directions:

1. Set together all the ingredients to a bowl and merge until combined. Serve immediately.

Nutrition: Calories: 550; Fat: 12g; Carbs: 85g; Protein: 25g

Thai Chicken Salad

Preparation time: 10 minutes

Cooking time: 15 minutes

Ingredients:

- 1 tablespoon olive oil, plus
- 2 teaspoons, divided
- 1/2 cup finely chopped red onion
- 1 teaspoon minced garlic
- 8 ounces boneless, skinless chicken breast

- 2 tablespoons freshly squeezed lime juice
- 1-inch piece fresh ginger, peeled and grated
- 1 teaspoon red pepper flakes
- 4 cups shredded Napa cabbage

- 1 cup snow peas
- 3/4 cup grated carrots
- 1/2 cup diced red bell pepper
- 1/4 cup chopped scallions
- 1/4 cup chopped fresh basil
- 1/4 cup chopped fresh cilantro
- 1/4 cup chopped cashews

Directions:

1. Heating 2 tablespoons of olive oil to medium-high heat in a big skillet. Cook the onion and garlic for two minutes with the attachment. Attach the chicken and cook it for 10 to 15 minutes, or until it is browned and the interior temperature reaches 165°F. After it has chilled, shred the poultry.
2. In a small bowl, set together the lime juice, ginger, and red pepper flakes. One tablespoon of the leftover olive oil should be whisked in gradually until combined.
3. Combine the cabbage, snow peas, carrots, bell pepper, scallions, basil, cilantro, and the chicken shreds in a sizable dish.
4. Add the dressing and toss. Divide between two serving bowls, top with the cashews, and serve.

Nutrition: Calories: 445; Fat: 21g; Carbs: 32g; Protein: 35g

Cauliflower Fried Rice

Preparation time: 15 minutes

Cooking time: 15 minutes

Ingredients:

- 1 head of cauliflower, riced
- 1 tbsp olive oil
- 1 small onion, diced
- 2 cloves of garlic, minced
- 1 cup frozen peas and carrots
- 2 eggs, lightly beaten
- 2 green onions, thinly sliced
- 2 tbsp soy sauce
- 1 tsp sesame oil
- Salt and pepper, to taste

Directions:

1. Pulse the florets of cauliflower in a food processor until they look like rice.
2. Heat the skillet and olive oil over medium heat until warmed. Attach the onion and garlic and process for about 5 minutes, until they are soft.

3. Attach frozen peas and carrots and cook for about 2-3 minutes, until they are no longer frozen.

4. Set the vegetables to one side of the pan and whisk the eggs on the other. Scramble the eggs until they are done, and then mix them with the vegetables.

5. Add cauliflower that has been riced, green onions, soy sauce, and sesame oil. Stir until the mixture has a velvety, smooth texture.

6. You can add salt and pepper to your preference.

7. Cook for about 5–7 minutes, or until the cauliflower is soft.

Nutrition: Calories: 273; Fat: 17g; Carbs: 22g; Protein: 12

Salmon with Creamy Feta Cucumbers

Preparation time: 5 minutes   Cooking time: 15 minutes

Ingredients:

- 4 salmon fillets2 tbsp. lemon juice
- 1 tbsp. olive oil
- Salt and pepper, to taste
- 1/2 cup of crumbled feta cheese

- 1/4 cup of sour cream
- 1/4 cup of sliced fresh dill
- 1/4 cup of sliced fresh mint
- 2 cucumbers, divided
- 2 cloves of garlic

Directions:

1. Set your oven to 400F (200C).

2. Merge feta, sour cream, olive oil, dill, mint, lemon juice, salt, and pepper in a small bowl.

3. Set the salmon fillets on a baking sheet sealed with parchment paper.

4. Spread the feta mixture evenly over the salmon fillets.

5. Bake in the oven for a duration of 10 to 12 minutes or until the salmon is done and the feta mixture is golden brown.

6. While the salmon is baking, slice the cucumbers and crush the garlic cloves.

7. In a separate pan, sauté the cucumbers and garlic in a bit of oil until the cucumbers are slightly softened.

8. Prepare the salmon with the cucumbers on the side.

Nutrition: Calories: 280; Fat: 12g; Carbs: 9g; Protein: 34g

Chicken Salad with Pistachios

Preparation time: 20 minutes   Cooking time: 30 minutes

Ingredients:

- Olive oil nonstick spray
- 1 cup peeled and sliced carrots
- 1/2 tablespoon brown sugar
- 3 teaspoons olive oil, divided
- 1/4 teaspoon salt, plus pinch, divided
- 1/4 tsp. freshly ground black pepper, plus pinch, divided
- 1 (6-ounce) boneless, skinless chicken breast, cut cross-wise into thin slices
- 4 tablespoons sliced scallions, divided
- 1 tablespoon apple cider vinegar
- 1/4 cup thinly sliced shallot
- 4 cups baby arugula
- 1 cup halved seedless red grapes
- 2 tablespoons unsalted shelled chopped pistachios

Directions:

1. Set the oven temperature to 425°F to preheat.
2. Coat a 9-by-9-inch baking pan and a rimmed baking sheet with olive oil cooking spray.
3. Put the vegetables to the baking dish that has been ready.
4. Add the brown sugar, 1 teaspoon of olive oil, 1/8 teaspoon of salt, and 1/8 teaspoon of pepper. Toss to evenly cover.
5. Roast the carrots for 25 minutes, giving them frequent stirs, or until they are soft and they margins are just beginning to turn golden.
6. Arrange the poultry on the preheated baking sheet in a mound about five minutes before the cooking period is up.
7. One teaspoon of olive oil should be drizzled over the dish before 2 tablespoons of scallions, the final 1/8 teaspoon of salt, and the leftover peppercorns are added. Mix by tossing.

8. Arrange everything in one row.

9. Cook for 6 minutes, rotating once, or until thoroughly cooked to an internal temperature of 165°F.

10. Remove the carrots and chicken from the device and let them chill for a few minutes.

11. In the meantime, assemble the vinegar, shallot, remaining 1 teaspoon of olive oil, remaining 2 tablespoons of scallions, and a pinch of salt and pepper in a sizable salad fish. Give it five minutes to stand so that the tastes can meld.

12. Whisk together the arugula and grapes in the large dish with the dressing and toss to combine.

13. Divide between two serving plates.

14. Top each plate with the carrots, chicken and any juices, and sprinkle each with 1 tablespoon of pistachios.

15. Serve warm.

Nutrition: Calories: 263; Fat: 10g; Carbs: 22g; Protein: 22g

Tilapia with Tomatoes and Pepper Relish

Preparation time: 15 minutes

Cooking time: 5 minutes

Ingredients:

- 4 tilapia fillets
- 1/2 tsp. salt
- 1/4 tsp. black pepper
- 2 tbsp. olive oil
- 2 red bell peppers, cored and diced
- 1 red onion, diced

- 2 cloves of garlic, minced
- 1 pint cherry tomatoes, halved
- 2 tbsp. red wine vinegar
- 1 tbsp. honey
- 2 tbsp. chopped fresh parsley or cilantro

Directions:

1. Season the tilapia fillets with salt and pepper.

2. Warm 1 tablespoon of olive oil in a skillet on medium-high heat until hot.

3. Heat 1 tbsp. of the olive oil in a skillet over medium-high heat.

4. Add the tilapia fillets and cook for 2-3 minutes each side, or until the fish is cooked through.
5. Detach from skillet and set aside.
6. Warmth the last tbsp. of olive oil in the same pan.
7. Add the onion, garlic, and bell peppers. Process the vegetables for 5- 6 minutes, or until they are soft.
8. Stir in the honey, red wine vinegar, and cherry tomatoes. Cook for a further 2 to 3 minutes, or until the tomatoes are slightly softer and heated through.
9. Stir in the chopped parsley or cilantro.
10. Serve the tilapia fillets with the pepper and tomato relish on top.

Nutrition: Calories: 385; Fat: 6g; Carbs: 1g; Protein: 8g

Simple Tomato Basil Soup

Preparation time: 5 minutes

Cooking time: 10 minutes

Ingredients:

- 1 cup sliced onion
- 4 garlic cloves
- 1 tbsp. olive oil
- 1/8 tbsp. salt
- 1 tbsp. freshly ground black pepper
- 7 cups sliced fresh tomatoes (aim for a mix of large, cherry, grape, and heirloom)
- 1/2 cup sliced fresh basil leaves

Directions:

1. In an iron saucepan over medium heat, warm the olive oil. For a few minutes to a minute, place the onion and garlic in the pan.
2. Stir in the tomatoes and cook them, turning occasionally, until they have softened and broken down.
3. Take it away from the fire and add the basil along with the salt and pepper.
4. Until smooth, merge in a mixer or with an immersion blender. Serve immediately.

Nutrition: Calories: 169; Fat: 4g; Carbs: 33g; Protein: 7g

Creamy Chicken and Chickpea Salad

Preparation time: 10 minutes   Cooking time: 0 minutes

Ingredients:

- 1 cup cubed cooked chicken breast
- 1 (7.5 ounce) can chickpeas, drained and rinsed
- 1 cup chopped seeded cucumber
- 1/4 cup chopped scallions
- 2 tablespoons chopped fresh mint
- 1 garlic clove, minced

- 1/4 cup plain nonfat Greek yogurt
- Pinch salt
- 2 cups baby spinach leaves
- 2 tablespoons sliced almonds
- 1 lemon, cut into wedges
- 1 medium tomato, cut into wedges

Directions:

1. Combine the chicken, chickpeas, cucumber, scallions, mint, garlic, yogurt, and salt and toss gently.
2. Gently fold in the spinach.
3. Divide the salad between two serving plates, top with the sliced almonds, place the lemon and tomato wedges on the side, and serve.

Nutrition: Calories: 390; Fat: 8g; Carbs: 42g; Protein: 41g

Seared Tilapia with Spiralized Zucchini

Preparation time: 10 minutes   Cooking time: 25 minutes

Ingredients:

- 4 Tilapia fillets
- 2 cloves of garlic, sliced
- 2 tbsp. butter
- To taste: Salt and pepper

- 2 tbsp. of olive oil
- 1 zucchini, spiralized
- Lemon wedges for serving

Directions:

1. Salt and pepper the tilapia fillets on both sides.
2. In a large skillet over medium-high heat, warm the olive oil. The Tilapia fillets should be cooked thoroughly and golden brown after 3–4 minutes on each side.
3. Remove the Tilapia from the skillet and set aside.
4. Add the spiralized zucchini, garlic, and butter to the same skillet. Process for 2-3 minutes or until the zucchini is crisp.
5. Take the Tilapia to the skillet and process for 1-2 minutes or until heated.
6. Serve the Tilapia and zucchini with lemon wedges on the side.

Nutrition: Calories: 289; Fat: 13g; Carbs: 7g; Protein: 36g

Broccoli and Gold Potato Soup

Preparation time: 10 minutes   Cooking time: 35 minutes

Ingredients:

- Ground black pepper
- 1/4 cup sliced fresh chives
- 1/2 cup sliced onion
- 2 cups broccoli florets
- 1 tbsp. olive oil
- 1/4 tbsp. dried thyme
- 1 garlic clove, sliced

- 3 cups low-sodium vegetable broth
- 1/4 tbsp. red pepper flakes
- Salt
- 2 cups peeled and chopped Yukon gold potatoes

Directions:

1. Set the olive oil in a saucepan over medium heat. Attach the onion and garlic and cook 4 or 5 minutes until fragrant and translucent.
2. Attach the vegetable broth and potatoes. Seal and bring to a boil. Set the heat to medium and cook for about 15 minutes.
3. Set the broccoli, thyme, and red pepper flakes, cover, and steam for 5 minutes, or until the broccoli is processed but still bright green.
4. Set the soup in a blender. Set with salt and pepper.

5. Ladle into bowls, garnish with the chives, and serve.

Nutrition: Calories: 268; Fat: 10g; Carbs: 35g; Protein: 13g

Braised Lentils and Vegetables

Preparation time: 15 minutes   Cooking time: 60 minutes

Ingredients:

- 1/2 tablespoon olive oil
- 3/4 cup diced onion
- 2 garlic cloves, minced
- 1 celery stalk, thinly sliced
- 4 ounces baby carrots
- 1/2 cup sliced mushrooms
- 1 fennel bulb, cut into 8 wedges
- 3/4 cup dried green French lentils du Puy (or brown lentils), rinsed well and drained

- 1/4 cup water
- 11/2 cups unsalted vegetable stock
- 2 fresh thyme sprigs
- 1 fresh rosemary sprig
- Salt
- Freshly ground black pepper
- Fresh parsley leaves, for garnish

Directions:

1. Heat a deep 4-quart saucepan over medium-high heat. Add the olive oil and heat for 20 to 30 seconds.
2. When the onion begins to soften and turn brown, add it, reduce the heat to medium, and continue processing for about 5 minutes.
3. Add the garlic and celery, stir periodically, and cook for an additional five minutes.
4. Add the carrots, mushrooms, fennel, lentils, and water and process for 2 to 3 minutes, stirring until the water is completely absorbed.
5. Include the broth, rosemary, and thyme.
6. Reduce the heat to medium and cover the pan to keep the food warm. Ideally, the liquid will scarcely simmer. Cook the lentils for 40 to 45 minutes, or until they are mostly incorporated into the liquid and neither too soft nor too firm. Serve with fresh cilantro as a garnish after seasoning with salt and pepper.

Nutrition: Calories: 399; Fat: 6g; Carbs: 64g; Protein: 26g

Acorn Squash Stuffed with White Beans

Preparation time: 10 minutes   Cooking time: 25 minutes

Ingredients:

- 1/8 tbsp. salt
- 1/4 tbsp. freshly ground black pepper, divided
- 1/4 cup sliced onion
- 1 cup canned white beans, washed and drained
- 2 tbsp. wheat germ
- 2 garlic cloves, minced
- 1 tbsp. water
- 1 tbsp. dried basil

- 1 tbsp. dried rosemary
- 21/2 tbsp. olive oil
- 4 cups stemmed and chopped kale
- 1 tbsp. tomato paste, no salt added
- 1 medium acorn squash, halved and seeded
- 2 tbsp. feta cheese

Directions:

1. To make each squash half lay level, cut a thin slice off the bottom. Sprinkle the salt and 1/8 teaspoon black pepper inside after brushing with 1/2 teaspoon of olive oil. Place in a microwave safe dish that is 8 by 8 inches. For about 12 minutes on high in the microwave, cover with plastic wrap and cook the zucchini until fork-tender.

2. In the interim, warm 1 teaspoon of olive oil in a pan. The onion should be added and cooked for two to three minutes while tossing, or until it begins to brown. For one minute, while tossing, add the garlic. Add the leftover 1/8 teaspoon of pepper and the water to the tomato paste.

3. When the kale is tender, stir it in, cover the pan, and simmer for 3 to 5 minutes, Add the beans and simmer for an additional 2 minutes. Get rid of the humidity.

4. Position the oven's middle shelf and turn on the broiler.

5. In a bowl, combine the wheat germ, basil, rosemary, feta cheese, and the remaining 1 teaspoon of olive oil. Each squash portion should be stuffed with half of the kale-bean mixture, Put them on a baking tray or in an ovenproof dish. Sprinkle them with the wheat germ mixture and simmer for 1 to 2 minutes, or until the wheat germ has browned. Serve warm.

Nutrition: Calories: 401; Fat: 10g; Carbs: 68g; Protein: 18g

Cheesy Artichoke Toasts

Preparation time: 10 minutes

Cooking time: 15 minutes

Ingredients:

- 1 can (14 oz) artichoke hearts, drained and chopped
- 1/4 cup mayonnaise
- 1/4 cup sour cream
- 1/4 cup grated Parmesan cheese
- 2 cloves of garlic, minced
- 1/4 tsp salt
- 1/4 tsp black pepper
- 1 baguette, sliced into 1/2-inch thick slices
- 1 cup shredded mozzarella cheese

Directions:

1. Preheat the oven to 425 degrees F (220 degrees C).
2. In a mixing bowl, combine the chopped artichoke hearts, mayonnaise, sour cream, Parmesan cheese, garlic, salt, and pepper. Mix well.
3. Slices of baguette should be arranged on a baking sheet.
4. Each baguette slice should have the artichoke mixture spread on it.
5. Sprinkle the artichoke mixture with mozzarella cheese that has been shredded.
6. Toasts should be golden brown and the cheese should be melted after 10 to 12 minutes in the oven.
7. Note: You can also add other ingredients to the artichoke mixture like chopped parsley, green onion, or red pepper flakes to give it more flavor.

Nutrition: Calories: 325; Fat: 15g; Carbs: 33g; Protein: 13g

Spring Minestrone Soup

Preparation time: 20 minutes

Cooking time: 40 minutes

Ingredients:

- tbsp olive oil
- one onion, diced
- two cloves of garlic, minced
- 1 cup diced carrots

- 1 cup diced celery
- 1 cup diced potatoes
- 1 cup fresh or frozen green peas
- 1 cup fresh or frozen corn
- 4 cups chicken or vegetable broth
- 2 cups water
- one can (14.5 oz) diced tomatoes
- 1 tsp dried basil
- 1 tsp dried oregano
- salt and pepper to taste
- one can (15 oz) cannellini beans, drained and rinsed
- 1/2 cup small pasta (such as ditalini or elbow macaroni)
- 2 cups chopped spinach or kale
- 1/4 cup grated Parmesan cheese (optional

Directions:

1. In a pot, set up the olive oil over medium heat.
2. For about 5 minutes, attach the onion and garlic and simmer until tender.
3. Attach the salt, pepper, broth, chopped tomatoes, water, basil, oregano, potatoes, carrots, celery, green peas, and corn.
4. When the vegetables are soft, simmer for 15 minutes after bringing to a boil.
5. Stir in the cannellini beans, pasta, and spinach/kale.
6. Boil for an additional 8-10 minutes or until pasta is cooked.
7. Set into bowls and sprinkle with grated Parmesan cheese if desired. Serve hot.

Nutrition: Calories: 376; Fat: 13g; Carbs: 54g; Protein: 16g

Lemon-Thyme Chicken

Preparation time: 5 minutes

Cooking time: 20 minutes

Ingredients:

- 4 boneless, chicken breasts2 tbsp. fresh thyme leaves
- 2 tbsp. fresh lemon juice 1/4 cup of chicken broth

- To taste: Salt and pepper
- 2 tbsp. of olive oil
- 2 cloves of garlic, sliced

Directions:

1. Set chicken breasts with salt and pepper.
2. Over medium-high heat, warm up the olive oil in a big skillet.
3. Cook the chicken breasts until golden brown and well cooked, about 5 to 6 minutes per side.
4. Set the chicken out of the pan and set it aside.
5. Attach thyme leaves and minced garlic to the same skillet.
6. Heat the ingredients until they become aromatic, for about 1 to 2 minutes.
7. Stir together the chicken stock and lemon juice in the skillet.
8. Simmer for a while.
9. Set the chicken in the skillet once more and top with the sauce.
10. Cook for a further 2 to 3 minutes, or until the chicken is thoroughly heated and the sauce has slightly thickened.
11. If preferred, top with extra thyme leaves and lemon wedges before serving.

Nutrition: Calories: 405; Fat: 15g; Carbs: 9g; Protein: 50

Roasted Garlic and Tomato Lentil Salad

Preparation time: 15 minutes   Cooking time: 30 minutes

Ingredients:

- 1 whole garlic bulb
- 1 tablespoon olive oil, plus 2 teaspoons, divided
- 1 cup halved grape tomatoes
- 1/2 cup sliced red onion
- Salt
- Freshly ground black pepper
- 1 cup low-sodium vegetable broth
- 1/2 cup green lentils
- 1/2 cup diced red bell pepper
- 1/4 cup diced celery
- 1/4 cup pumpkin seeds
- 1/4 cup finely chopped fresh parsley
- 1 tablespoon freshly squeezed lemon juice
- Pinch red pepper flakes

Directions:

1. Preheat the oven to 375°F and cover a baking sheet with parchment paper.

2. Cut the top off the garlic bulb and place it on a small piece of aluminum foil. Drizzle the bulb with 1 teaspoon of olive oil and close the foil around the garlic.

3. Place the tomatoes and onion on the baking tray that has been preheated. Drizzle with 1 teaspoon of olive oil. Add the salt and pepper to taste.

4. Bake the veggies and the wrapped garlic for 25 to 30 minutes, or until the vegetables are slightly shriveled.

5. Bring the broth to a boil in a big saucepan in the meantime. Add the lentils, decrease the heat, cover, and simmer for 20 to 25 minutes, or until tender. Drain and bring to a bowl.

6. Carefully open the garlic packet and allow the garlic to cool. Gently press the cloves from the bulb into a small bowl and use the back of a fork to break up the garlic into smaller pieces.

7. Add the garlic, baked tomatoes and onion, bell pepper, celery, pumpkin seeds, and parsley to the lentils.

8. Stir the lemon juice, red pepper flakes, and one tablespoon of olive oil in a small bowl. Add salt and pepper. Toss the dressing with the lentil mixture and serve.

Nutrition: Calories: 368; Fat: 21g; Carbs: 33g; Protein: 16g

Grilled Chicken and Cherry Salad

Preparation time: 30 minutes   Cooking time: 10 minutes

Ingredients:

- 4 skinless, boneless chicken breasts
- To taste: Salt and pepper
- 1/4 cup of olive oil
- A quarter cup balsamic vinegar
- 2 cloves garlic, chopped

- 1/4 cup minced fresh basil
- 2 cups fresh cherries, pitted and divided
- 2 cups mixed green veggies
- Feta cheese crumbles, ¼ cup

Directions:

1. Sprinkle salt and pepper on the chicken meat breasts.

2. Set the grill to medium-high heat. Grill the chicken for 6 to 8 minutes on each side, or until completely cooked.

3. In a small dish, whisk together the basil, garlic, balsamic vinegar, and olive oil.

4. After the chicken has fully cooked, let it cool for a while before slicing.

5. Arrange mixed greens on a platter or plates and top with sliced chicken, cherries, and feta cheese.

6. Pour dressing over the lettuce before serving.

Nutrition: Calories: 243; Fat: 12g; Carbs: 16g; Protein: 20g

Creamy Asparagus Pea Soup

Preparation time: 5 minutes

Cooking time: 25 minutes

Ingredients:

For the soup

- 1 large bundle asparagus, trimmed
- 2 tsp. olive oil, plus more for drizzling
- Salt
- Freshly ground black pepper

- 2 garlic cloves, minced
- 1/3 cup thinly sliced shallots
- 1 cup fresh or frozen peas
- 11/2 cups plain soy milk
- 11/2 cups low-sodium vegetable broth

For the garlic herb croutons

- 1/8 tbsp. garlic powder
- 1 tbsp. olive oil
- 1/8 tbsp. freshly ground black pepper
- 1 cup cubed whole-grain bread

- 1/8 tbsp. dried oregano
- 1/8 tbsp. dried basil
- Grated parmesan cheese, for topping (optional)

Directions:

To make the soup

1. Switch on the oven to 400°F.

2. On a baking pan, spread the asparagus out evenly. Sprinkle with a drizzle of olive oil and a gentle sprinkle of salt and pepper. Coat by tossing.

3. After 15 minutes or roasting, set it away. To 325°F, drop the oven's temperature.

4. In a big saucepan, heat 2 tablespoons of olive oil over medium heat. When translucent and aromatic, set the shallots and garlic and cook for 2 to 3 minutes.

5. Include the peas, soy milk, and veggie broth. Set salt and pepper to taste. Give to a boil, then reduce the heat to a simmer for five minutes.

6. Combine the broth and roasted asparagus in a blender, and process until very smooth and creamy. Refill the saucepan with the soup, then stew it there for a while.

To make the garlic herb croutons

1. Whisk together the bread pieces in a sizable bowl for mixing. Combine the olive oil, pepper, oregano, basil, garlic powder, and pepper in a small dish. Divide the mixture over the bread pieces. Cover by tossing.

2. Put together the bread pieces in a single layer on a clean baking sheet and bake for 15 to 20 minutes or until golden brown, For even grilling, stir after 10 minutes.

3. Ladle the soup into plates, add some black pepper, some croutons, and Parmesan cheese and serve.

Nutrition: Calories: 393; Fat: 17g; Carbs: 44g; Protein: 20g

Pork Fried Rice

Preparation time: 15 minutes   Cooking time: 20 minutes

Ingredients:

- 2 cups cooked white rice, cooled
- 1/2 lb. pork, sliced into small pieces
- 1 tbsp. vegetable oil1/2 cup of frozen peas
- 2 eggs, beaten
- 3 tbsp. soy sauce
- 2 tbsp. oyster sauce
- 2 cloves of garlic, sliced
- 1/2 cup minced onions
- 1/2 cup chopped carrots
- 1 tsp. sesame oil
- Salt and pepper to taste

Directions:

1. Heat the pan on a medium-high flame and add the vegetable oil.
2. Add the pork and simmer for 5 - 7 minutes, or until browned.
3. Attach the garlic, onions, carrots, and frozen peas to the pan.
4. Process until the vegetables are softened, about 5-7 minutes.
5. Push the pork and vegetables to the side of the pan and pour in the beaten eggs.
6. Scramble the eggs until cooked through.
7. Toss in the cooked rice after adding it to the skillet with the vegetables and meat.
8. Pour in the soy sauce, oyster sauce, and sesame oil.
9. Set to coat the rice evenly.
10. Flavor with salt and pepper to taste.
11. Serve the pork fried rice warm.

Nutrition: Calories: 357; Fat: 14g; Carbs: 34g; Protein: 24g

Chicken Satay

Preparation time: 30 minutes   Cooking time: 10 minutes

Ingredients:

- Coconut oil for greasing
- 1 cup shredded zucchini
- 1 cup cauliflower rice
- 2 scallions, thinly sliced
- ¼ cup coconut flour
- ¼ tsp sea salt
- 3 tbsp coconut oil

Directions:

1. Slice the chicken thighs into bite-sized pieces.
2. Merge the coconut milk, brown sugar, soy sauce, cumin, coriander, turmeric, and cayenne pepper in a small bowl.
3. Combine the ginger, garlic, and peanut butter in a separate little bowl.
4. Spill the coconut milk mixture over the chicken in a bowl. Toss to evenly coat the chicken.
5. Chicken skewers are threaded onto them.

6. To medium-high heat, set a grill or grill pan.

7. The chicken skewers should be cooked through after grilling for around 5-7 minutes on each side.

8. Serve the chicken skewers with the peanut sauce on the side.

Nutrition: Calories: 117; Fat: 6g; Carbs: 26g; Protein: 12g

Easy Fried Eggplant

Preparation time: 20 minutes   Cooking time: 15 minutes

Ingredients:

- 1 large eggplant, sliced into rounds
- Salt
- 1 cup all-purpose flour
- 2 eggs, beaten
- 1 cup breadcrumbs
- Oil for frying

Directions:

1. Cut the eggplant into thin, uniform slices and sprinkle with salt.

2. Allow the food to sit for 30 minutes to reduce its bitterness.

3. Slices of eggplant should be washed and dried with paper towels.

4. Create a breading station with three shallow bowls: one for the breadcrumbs, one for the beaten eggs, and one for the flour.

5. Each eggplant slice should be dipped in flour, beaten eggs, and then breadcrumbs, pressing the breadcrumbs into the slices to help them stick.

6. In a skillet, warmth the oil over medium-high heat.

7. When the oil is hot, attach the breaded eggplant slices and cook for 3-4 minutes each side.

8. With a slotted spoon, detach the eggplant slices from the oil and set them on a tray sealed with paper towels to drain.

9. Serve the fried eggplant warm.

Nutrition: Calories: 357; Fat: 14g; Carbs: 46g; Protein: 13g

Simple Lemon-Herb Chicken

Preparation time: 5 minutes

Cooking time: 10 minutes

Ingredients:

- 4 boneless, chicken breasts
- 1/4 cup of fresh lemon juice
- 2 cloves of garlic, sliced
- 1 tsp. dried thyme
- To taste: Salt and pepper

- 1/4 cup of all-purpose flour
- 2 tbsp. olive oil
- 1/4 cup of chicken broth
- 1 tsp. dried basil
- 1/4 cup sliced fresh

Directions:

1. Chicken breasts are floured and then set with salt and pepper.
2. Add the olive oil to a big skillet set over medium-high flame.
3. The chicken breasts should be fried for 4-5 minutes on each side, or until golden brown and cooked properly, once the oil is heated.
4. Detach the chicken from the skillet and set it away.
5. Fill the same pan with the chicken stock, lemon juice, garlic, thyme, and basil.
6. Boil the combination for 2 to 3 minutes, or until the sauce has thickened.
7. Before adding the poultry back to the skillet, spoon some sauce over it.
8. Cook the chicken for an additional 2 to 3 minutes, or until it is properly cooked.
9. Add fresh cilantro as a garnish and serve.

Nutrition: Calories: 212; Fat: 9g; Carbs: 8g; Protein: 29g

Rustic Vegetable and Bean Soup

Preparation time: 10 minutes

Cooking time: 15 minutes

Ingredients:

- 1 tablespoon olive oil
- 1/2 cup chopped celery
- 1/2 cup chopped shallots

- Salt
- Freshly ground black pepper
- 2 garlic cloves, minced

- 1 tablespoon chopped fresh marjoram
- 1/2 cup chopped carrots
- 1/2 cup peeled and diced gold potatoes
- 1/2 cup chopped tomatoes, with juices reserved
- 3 cups low-sodium vegetable broth, divided
- 1 can navy beans, drained and rinsed
- 2 teaspoons red wine vinegar
- 1/4 cup thinly sliced chives, for garnish

Directions:

1. Set the olive oil in a 4-quart soup pot over medium heat.
2. Set the celery and shallots and season with salt and black pepper.
3. Frequently stir the veggies until they start to soften.
4. Attach the garlic and marjoram and cook until fragrant, 1 minute more.
5. Add the carrots, potatoes, and tomatoes, stirring to incorporate with the seasonings and aromatics, then boil the vegetables in 2 cups of broth while partially covering the pot, until they are just about tender, usually for 10 to 20 minutes.
6. Include the legumes, tomato juices that have been set aside, and the final cup of broth.
7. Stir to incorporate, then simmer the flavors for 10 minutes with a partial cover.
8. Ladle the soup into bowls, add chives to each cup, and serve.

Nutrition: Calories: 472; Fat: 10g; Carbs: 69g; Protein: 28g

Easy Chorizo Street Tacos

Preparation time: 10 minutes   Cooking time: 10 minutes

Ingredients:

- 1 pound Mexican chorizo, casing removed
- 1/2 cup diced onion
- 1/2 cup diced bell pepper
- Salt and pepper to taste
- Corn tortillas
- Toppings of your choice such as cilantro, diced onion, diced

tomatoes, sour cream, and lime
wedges

Directions:

1. Cook the chorizo for 5-7 minutes, stirring occasionally, until browned in a large skillet over medium-high heat.
2. To the skillet, attach the bell pepper and onion dice. Process for about 5 minutes, or until softened.
3. Set the chorizo mixture with salt and pepper.
4. In a separate skillet, heat the corn tortillas over medium heat until warm and slightly charred.
5. To assemble the tacos, set a few spoonfuls of the chorizo mixture onto each tortilla, and top with your desired toppings.
6. Serve the tacos warm.

Nutrition: Calories: 262; Fat: 13g; Carbs: 26g; Protein: 10g

Moroccan Spiced Red Lentils Stew

Preparation time: 15 minutes

Cooking time: 50 minutes

Ingredients:

- 3 cups low-sodium vegetable broth
- Salt
- 1/3 cup dry millet
- 1/2 tbsp. olive oil
- 2 tbsp. tomato paste
- 1/8 tbsp. cayenne pepper
- 1 cup dried lentils, rinsed
- 1/2 cup finely sliced onion
- 1/2 cup finely sliced red bell pepper
- 1 celery stalks, sliced
- 1/4 tbsp. ground cinnamon
- 1/2 cup sliced dried apricots
- 1 tbsp. ground coriander
- 1/2 tbsp. ground cumin

Directions:

1. In a 3-quart stockpot or skillet, heat the olive oil over medium heat.

Attach the onion, and cook it for about 6 minutes, turning frequently, until it is fragrant.

). Provide the millet, legumes, and broth. The mixture should boil.

4. Put in the dried apricots, cayenne, coriander, cumin, tomato puree, bell pepper, celery, and salt to taste.

5. Lower the heat, cover the pot, and let the lentils and millet cook for 35 to 45 minutes, or until they are tender. Serve hot.

Nutrition: Calories: 573; Fat: 7g; Carbs: 96g; Protein: 33g

Garlic Ranch Chicken

Preparation time: 10 minutes   Cooking time: 20 minutes

Ingredients:

- 4 boneless, chicken breasts
- 1/2 cup of buttermilk
- 1 tsp. dried chives
- 1 tsp. onion powder
- 1/2 tsp. salt
- 1/4 tsp. black pepper
- 1/4 cup of all-purpose flour

- 1/4 cup of mayonnaise
- 2 cloves of garlic, sliced
- 2 tbsp. sliced fresh parsley
- 1 tbsp. chopped fresh dill
- 1/4 cup of olive oil or vegetable oil

Directions:

1. In a large bowl, merge the buttermilk, parsley, mayonnaise, garlic, onion powder, dill, chives, salt, and pepper.
2. Put the chicken breasts in the bowl and toss them around so that the marinade covers them evenly. For best results, cover and put in the fridge for at least an hour or overnight.
3. Put the flour in a shallow dish.
4. Take the chicken breasts out of the marinade and let the excess drip off. Then set the flour to coat the chicken breasts.
5. Warm up the oil in a large pan over medium heat.

6. When the oil is hot, attach the chicken breasts and cook 8 minutes per side, or until they are golden brown and processed all the way through.

7. Take the chicken out of the pan and put it on a plate lined with paper towels to soak up any extra oil.

8. Serve the chicken with your favorite sides, like roasted vegetables, mashed potatoes, or a salad.

Nutrition: Calories: 264; Fat: 12g; Carbs: 7g; Protein: 30g

Flounder Tacos with Cabbage Slaw

Preparation time: 10 minutes

Cooking time: 6 minutes

Ingredients:

- 2 tbsp. freshly squeezed lime juice
- 1 cup thinly sliced red cabbage
- 1/2 avocado, chopped
- 3 tbsp. olive oil, divided
- 1 tbsp. ground cumin

- 8 ounces skinless flounder fillets, sliced into 1-inch chunks
- 4 corn tortillas, warmed
- 1/8 tbsp. salt
- 1/8 tbsp. freshly ground black pepper
- Fresh cilantro, for garnish

Directions:

1. In a small bowl, merge together the flounder, cumin, salt, and pepper.
2. In another small bowl, mix together the cabbage, avocado, lime juice, and 1 teaspoon of olive oil.
3. In a medium-sized pan over medium-high heat, warm the final 2 teaspoons of olive oil.
4. When the flounder is nearly opaque and flakes readily with a fork, add it to the skillet and cook, turning occasionally, for about 4 minutes.
5. Arrange two warm tortillas on each dish and top with the cabbage avocado slaw after dividing the salmon among them.
6. Serve with fresh cilantro as a topping.

Nutrition: Calories: 413; Fat: 20g; Carbs: 28g; Protein: 32g

Easy Baked Tilapia

Preparation time: 5 minutes

Cooking time: 25 minutes

Ingredients:

- 4 Tilapia fillets
- Salt and pepper to taste
- 2 tablespoons olive oil
- 2 cloves of garlic, minced
- 2 tablespoons lemon juice
- 1/4 cup chopped fresh parsley

Directions:

1. Set the oven's temperature to 375°F.
2. Tilapia fillets should be salted and peppered.
3. Combine the olive oil, parsley, lemon juice, and garlic in a small bowl.
4. Tilapia fillets should be set in a baking dish, and the olive oil mixture should be brushed over the fish.
5. When the Tilapia is processed through and flaky, bake it in the preheated oven for 10 to 15 minutes.
6. Prepare the baked Tilapia with your desired sides such as roasted vegetables, rice, or a salad.

Nutrition: Calories: 172; Fat: 4g; Carbs: 7g; Protein: 25g

Tuna Fish Pea Salad

Preparation time: 5 minutes

Cooking time: 10 minutes

Ingredients:

- One can of tuna fish, drained
- 1 cup of thawed frozen peas
- 1/4 cup of minced onion
- 1/4 cup of mayonnaise
- One tbsp. of lemon juice
- To taste: Salt and pepper

Directions:

1. In a large bowl, merge the tuna fish, peas, and onion.

2. In a small dish, merge the mayonnaise, lemon juice, salt, and pepper.

3. Pour mayonnaise mixture over the tuna and pea mixture.

4. Gently toss the ingredients to combine them.

5. Cover the bowl and put it in the fridge for at least 30 minutes to let the flavors mix.

6. Serve on a bed of lettuce or as a sandwich filling.

Nutrition: Calories: 103; Fat: 1g; Carbs: 7g; Protein: 17g

Loaded Sweet Potatoes

Preparation time: 5 minutes   Cooking time: 80 minutes

Ingredients:

- 1/2 avocado, peeled, seeded, and sliced
- 1/3 cup water
- 1 garlic clove, minced
- 1 can black beans
- salt

- 2 medium sweet potatoes
- 1/2 tbsp. olive oil
- 4 cups stemmed and chopped kale leaves
- 1/2 cup halved grape tomatoes
- Black pepper

Directions:

1. Cover a baking pan with parchment paper in the oven and warm the oven to 375°F.

2. Make several incisions in both sweet potatoes with a fork. The sweet potatoes should be baked for 45 to 60 minutes, or until they are soft.

3. Warm the olive oil in a medium pot over medium heat in the interim. Keep an eye out for browning as you attach the garlic and heat it for one minute, or until fragrant. Toss in the greens and tomatoes after adding them. Cook for 5 minutes after adding the water and covering.

4. Cook the veggies, stirring occasionally, for another 15 minutes, with the lid off, or until they are tender but still bright green.

5. Include the legumes and heat through. Add salt and pepper.

6. Divide the sweet potatoes into two equal parts lengthwise.

7. Top with the black bean-kale mixture and sliced avocado.

8. Serve hot.

Nutrition: Calories: 751; Fat: 15g; Carbs: 133g; Protein: 28g

Creamy Quinoa, Lentils, and Vegetables

Preparation time: 15 minutes   Cooking time: 45 minutes

Ingredients:

For the lentils

- 1/4 cup dried black lentils
- 3/4 cup water
-

- Pinch salt

For the roasted carrots and beets

- 1/2 pound rainbow carrots with stems (stems optional)
- Olive oil nonstick cooking spray

- 2 medium beets, peeled and sliced
- Salt
- Freshly ground black pepper

For the creamy quinoa

- 3/4 cup low-sodium vegetable broth
- 3/4 cup unsweetened almond milk, divided
- 1/2 cup quinoa, rinsed
- 1/2 teaspoon onion powder
- 1/4 teaspoon garlic powder

- 1 cup chopped and stemmed
- Swiss chard
- 1 tbsp. chopped fresh parsley, plus more for garnish
- Salt
- Freshly ground black pepper
- 1/4 cup chopped almonds

Directions:

1. To make the lentils

In a saucepan over medium heat, set together the lentils, water, and salt and set to a boil. Seal, lower the heat to medium-low, and simmer for 35 to 40 minutes.

To make the roasted carrots and beets

1. Set the oven temperature to 400°F and prepare the baking sheet by lining it with a sheet of parchment paper.
2. Wash the carrots well and remove extra roots and leaves, leaving roughly 2 inches of stem.
3. Lightly spray the lined baking sheet with cooking spray, add the carrots and beets, then spray them lightly with cooking spray.
4. Whisk with salt and pepper to season. Toast for 25 to 30 minutes, or until the vegetables are fork-tender and beginning to brown.

To make the creamy quinoa

1. In a large, partly covered pan over medium heat, combine the vegetable broth, 1/4 cup of almond milk, quinoa, onion powder, and garlic powder.
2. Set the heat to medium, bring to a boil, and then simmer the quinoa for 15 to 20 minutes, or until it is tender.
3. Continue cooking and stirring while adding the final 1/4 cup of almond milk.
4. When all the milk is added and the quinoa has a light creaminess to it, add the cooked lentils, chard, and parsley.
5. Set off the heat and stir until the chard is slightly wilted.
6. Add salt and pepper.
7. Divide between two bowls, top with the roasted vegetables and almonds, garnish with parsley, and serve.

Nutrition: Calories: 445; Fat: 11g; Carbs: 70g; Protein: 20

Shrimp and Rice Noodle Salad

Preparation time: 15 minutes   Cooking time: 5 minutes

Ingredients:

- 8 oz. rice noodles
- 1 lb. large shrimp, peeled and deveined
- Two cloves garlic, sliced

- 2 tbsp. of fish sauce
- 2 tbsp. of rice vinegar
- 2 tbsp. brown sugar
- 1 tbsp. of soy sauce

- 1/4 tsp. red pepper flakes
- 1/4 cup sliced fresh cilantro
- 1/4 cup minced fresh mint
- 1/4 cup sliced fresh basil
- 1/4 cup minced peanuts
- 1/4 cup sliced green onions
- Slices of lime for serving

Directions:

1. Rice noodles should be prepared as instructed on the box.
2. Heat a little oil in a big skillet over medium-high heat.
3. Add the shrimp and garlic, and sauté for 2 to 3 minutes on each side, until the shrimp are perfectly cooked and pink.
4. Stir the red pepper flakes, fish sauce, rice vinegar, brown sugar, and soy sauce in a small dish.
5. Arrange the cooked noodles, shrimp, basil, mint, cilantro, peanuts, and green onions in a big dish.
6. Garnish the lettuce with the dressing, then toss it all together.

Nutrition: Calories: 273; Fat: 6.1g; Carbs: 36.9g; Protein: 16.8

SALAD RECIPES

Roasted New Red Potatoes

Preparation time: 5 minutes

Cooking time: 20 minutes

Ingredients:

- 1 lb. new red potatoes, washed and dried
- 2 tbsp. olive oil
- 1 tsp. dried thyme
- Salt and pepper, to taste

Directions:

1. Preheat the oven, set the temperature to 425 degrees Fahrenheit.
2. Slice the potatoes into wedges, roughly 1/2 inch in thickness.
3. In a large bowl, toss the potatoes with the olive oil, thyme, salt, and pepper until evenly coated.
4. Set the potatoes on a baking sheet in a single line.
5. Crisp for 20-25 minutes, or until the potatoes are tender and golden brown, flipping halfway through cooking.

Nutrition: Calories: 169; Fat: 7g; Carbs: 27g; Protein: 3g

Potato Dumplings

Preparation time: 20 minutes

Cooking time: 45 minutes

Ingredients:

- 4 cups mashed potatoes
- 1/2 cup all-purpose flour
- 1 egg
- 1/4 cup grated onion
- 2 cloves of garlic, minced
- 1 teaspoon salt
- 1/4 teaspoon black pepper
- 1/4 cup chopped fresh parsley
- Flour for dusting
- Water or chicken broth for boiling

Directions:

1. Merge the mashed potatoes, grated onion, flour, egg, grated garlic, salt, pepper, and parsley in a sizable mixing basin. Merge thoroughly.
1. Create 1 1/2-inch balls out of the mixture. They're delicately dusted with flour.
2. Large saucepan of water or chicken stock should be brought to a simmer.
3. Drop the dumplings gently into the soup or boiling water. Don't overcrowd the pot, please.
4. The dumplings need to float to the top after 8 to 10 minutes of cooking.
5. Using a slotted spoon, remove the dumplings from the water and set them on a dish covered in paper towels so that any extra water can drain off.
6. You can also fry the dumplings for a crispy exterior.

Nutrition: Calories: 277; Fat: 10g; Carbs: 42g; Protein: 6g

Marinated Carrot Salad

Preparation time: 20 minutes   Cooking time: 10 minutes

Ingredients:

- 4 cups of thinly sliced carrots
- 1/2 cup of white wine vinegar
- 1/4 cup of olive oil
- Two cloves of garlic, minced
- One teaspoon of honey
- One teaspoon of Dijon mustard
- Salt and pepper, to taste
- Fresh parsley or cilantro, chopped (optional)

Directions:

1. In a dish, set the sliced carrots.
2. In a separate dish, merge together the white wine vinegar, olive oil, garlic, honey, Dijon mustard, salt, and pepper.
3. Dijon mustard, salt, and pepper.
4. Drizzle the marinade on top of the carrots and mix together.

5. Cover the bowl and put it in the fridge for at least two hours so the carrots can soak up the flavors.

6. Before serving, remove it from the refrigerator and let it sit for about 15 minutes.

7. Garnish with fresh parsley or cilantro if desired.

8. Serve chilled or at room temperature.

Nutrition: Calories: 166; Fat: 8g; Carbs: 24g; Protein: 2g

Tofu Salad

Preparation time: 15 minutes   Cooking time: 30 minutes

Ingredients:

- One block of firm tofu, cubed after drained
- 1/4 cup of sliced red bell pepper
- 1/4 cup of mince cucumber
- 1/4 cup of chopped red onion
- Two tbsp. of rice vinegar
- Two tbsp. of soy sauce
- 1 tbsp. of sesame oil
- 1 tsp. of grated ginger
- 1 clove of garlic, mashed
- To taste: Salt and pepper
- Garnishes: sesame seeds and chopped green onions (optional)

Directions:

1. Strain the tofu to squeeze out any extra water. Make blocks out of it next.
2. Merge the tofu, bell pepper, cucumber, and onion in a sizable dish.
3. In a small dish, whisk together the rice vinegar, soy sauce, sesame oil, ginger, garlic, salt, and pepper.
4. Set the dressing over the tofu mixture and toss to merged.
5. Cover the bowl and put it in the fridge for at least 30 minutes so the flavors can mix.
6. Before serving, remove it from the refrigerator and let it sit for about 15 minutes.
7. If you want, you can add sesame seeds and chopped green onions.
8. Serve chilled or at room temperature.

Nutrition: Calories: 145; Fat: 9g; Carbs: 10g; Protein: 8g

Tomato Cucumber Salad

Preparation time: 10 minutes   Cooking time: 5 minutes

Ingredients:

- 2 cups of diced tomatoes
- 1 cup of diced cucumber
- 1/4 cup of diced red onion
- Two tablespoons of red wine vinegar
- One tablespoon of olive oil

- One teaspoon of honey
- One clove of garlic, minced
- Salt and pepper, to taste
  Fresh basil or parsley, chopped (optional)

Directions:

1. Toss the potatoes and other seasonings with the sauce after that.
2. Whisk the honey, garlic, salt, pepper, and red wine vinegar together in a small bowl.
3. Pour the dressing over the tomatoes and mix it all together.
4. Cover the bowl and put it in the fridge for at least 30 minutes so the flavors can mix.
5. Take it out of the fridge and let it cool for about 15 minutes before serving.
6. If you want, you can decorate with fresh basil or parsley.

Nutrition: Calories: 104; Fat: 8g; Carbs: 7g; Protein: 2g

Quinoa Spinach Power Salad

Preparation time: 5 minutes   Cooking time: 10 minutes

Ingredients:

- 2 cups finely sliced spinach
- 1 cup sugar snap peas
- 11/2 tbsp. of olive oil

- 1/4 tbsp. of salt
- 3/4 cup of diced tomato

- 11/2 tbsp. of freshly squeezed lemon juice
- 1/2 cup of diced cucumbers
- 1/4 cup of sliced almonds
- 2 cups of water
- 1/2 cup of uncooked quinoa, rinsed and drained
- 1/4 tbsp. of freshly ground black pepper

Directions:

1. Bring the water in a medium pot to a boil. Add the quinoa and keep boiling for 10 minutes or until the quinoa is soft.
2. Drain the quinoa and let it cool.
3. Put together the spinach, peas, tomato, cucumber, almonds, and cooled quinoa in a sizable dish.
4. Combine the lemon juice, olive oil, salt, and pepper in a small dish. Toss to coat after setting over the vegetables.
5. Divide between two serving bowls and enjoy.

Nutrition: Calories: 322; Fat: 18g; Carbs: 32g; Protein: 11g

Salad of Kale, Avocado, and Carrots

Preparation time: 10 minutes

Cooking time: 30 minutes

Ingredients:

- 1/8 tbsp. of salt
- 1/8 tbsp. of freshly ground black pepper
- 4 cups of stemmed and coarsely chopped kale
- 1/2 (15-ounce) can of chickpeas, drained and rinsed
- 1 large ripe of avocado, peeled, pitted, and cubed
- 2 tbsp. coarsely of chopped walnuts
- 1 cup of baby carrots, halved lengthwise
- 1 tbsp. of olive oil
- 2 tbsp. of freshly squeezed lemon juice

Directions:

1. Set the oven temperature to 400° F to preheat.
2. Mix up the carrots, olive oil, salt, and pepper in a small dish.
3. Place on a baking pan with a rim and bake for 20 minutes.
4. Return the baking tray in the oven once more after adding the chickpeas and walnuts.
5. Bake the carrots for an additional 5 to 10 minutes, or until they are golden and soft.
6. For about two minutes, rub the kale with your palms until it softens and turns bright green.
7. Combine the kale, lemon juice, and half of the avocado in a large serving dish.
8. Put together the spinach with half of the carrot mixture, then toss.
9. Add avocado and the leftover carrot mixture on top.
10. Distribute among two serving dishes and savor.

Nutrition: Calories: 535; Fat: 30g; Carbs: 58g; Protein: 17g

Fruit Punch Salad

Preparation time: 10 minutes   Cooking time: 5 minutes

Ingredients:

- One can of fruit cocktail, drained
- One can of pineapple chunks, drained
- One banana, sliced
- 1 cup of mini marshmallows
- 1/2 cup of shredded coconut
- 1/2 cup of sour cream
- 1/4 cup of sugar
- 1/4 cup of orange juice
- One tablespoon of lemon juice

Directions:

1. Mix the fruit cocktail, pineapple chunks, banana, marshmallows, and shredded coconut together in a large bowl.

2. Mix the sour cream, sugar, orange juice, and lemon juice in a separate small bowl.

3. Pour sour cream mixture over the fruit mixture and stir to mix.

4. Cover the bowl and put it in the fridge for at least 2 hours so the flavors can mix.

5. Please take it out of the fridge and allow it to sit for approximately 15 minutes before serving. Serve chilled.

6. Feel free to add other fruits of your choice, such as strawberries, blueberries, or any berry you like.

Nutrition: Calories: 69; Fat: 0g; Carbs: 17g; Protein: 1g

Avocado and Eggs Salad

Preparation time: 5 minutes

Cooking time: 10 minutes

Ingredients:

- Four large eggs
- Salt and pepper, to taste
- One tablespoon of butter or oil
- 4 cups mixed greens (arugula, spinach, or lettuce)
- One avocado, diced
- 1/4 cup cherry tomatoes, halved
- 1/4 cup red onion, thinly sliced
- Two tablespoons of balsamic vinegar
- One tablespoon of olive oil
- One teaspoon honey
- One clove of garlic, minced
- 1/4 teaspoon Dijon mustard

Directions:

1. In a saucepan, set a pot of water to a boil. Carefully lower the eggs into the water using a slotted spoon.

2. If you want soft-boiled eggs, stew them for 6–8 minutes; if you wish to hard-boiled eggs, simmer them for 10–12 minutes.

3. The eggs should be taken out of the water and cooled in an ice bath.

4. In a skillet, warmth the oil or butter over medium heat.

5. When the mixed greens are just beginning to wilt, add them to the skillet and cook for one to two minutes.

6. In a small bowl, combine the balsamic vinegar, olive oil, honey, garlic, and Dijon mustard. The cooked greens, avocado, cherry tomatoes, and red onion should all be combined in a big bowl.

7. Over the salad, set the dressing, and toss just enough to mix.

8. The cooled eggs should be peeled and divided into wedges.

9. Place the eggs over the top of the salad and flavor with salt and pepper.

Nutrition: Calories: 176; Fat: 13g; Carbs: 8g; Protein: 9g

Gingered Beef and Broccoli Salad Bowl

Preparation time: 20 minutes   Cooking time: 10 minutes

Ingredients:

- 1 pound flank steak
- 1/4 cup soy sauce
- Two tablespoons rice vinegar
- Two tablespoons brown sugar
- Two tablespoons grated ginger
- Two cloves garlic, minced
- Two tablespoons cornstarch
- Two tablespoons vegetable oil
- 4 cups broccoli florets
- 2 cups cooked brown rice

Directions:

1. Set together the rice vinegar, soy sauce, brown sugar, ginger, and garlic in a large dish.

2. Add the flank steak and turn it around to coat. Secure the meat and place it in the fridge for at least 30 minutes.

3. Merge 2 tbsp. of water with 2 tbsp. of corn flour in a shallow bowl to make a slurry.

4. In a large pan or wok set over high heat, heat the vegetable oil.

5. Drain the steak from the marinade, then add it to the pan. Process the steak for 2 to 3 minutes on each side, or until it's processed the way you like it.

6. Take the steak out of the pan and let it sit for a few minutes before cutting across the grain.

7. In the same skillet, add the broccoli florets and cook until they are tender and slightly charred.

8. To serve, set the cooked rice among bowls and set with the steak and broccoli.

Nutrition: Calories: 237; Fat: 9g; Carbs: 17g; Protein: 22g

Spinach, Pears, and Cranberries Salad

Preparation time: 15 minutes

Cooking time: 5 minutes

Ingredients:

- 6 cups fresh spinach leaves
- 1/4 cup sliced red onion
- 1/4 cup crumbled blue cheese
- 1/4 cup dried cranberries
- Two ripe pears, cored and diced

- 1/4 cup balsamic vinegar
- 1/4 cup olive oil
- One clove of garlic, minced
- Salt and pepper to taste

Directions:

1. Mix the spinach, red onion, blue cheese, dried cranberries, and diced pears in a large salad bowl.
2. Put the balsamic vinegar, olive oil, garlic, salt, and pepper in a small dish.
3. Splash the lettuce with the dressing, then swirl to spread it.
4. Let salad sit for a few minutes to give the spinach a chance to soften up a bit.
5. Present and savor!

Nutrition: Calories: 214; Fat: 11g; Carbs: 25g; Protein: 5g

Zucchini Patties

Preparation time: 20 minutes

Cooking time: 10 minutes

Ingredients:

- 2 medium zucchini, grated
- 1/2 cup grated onion

- 1/2 cup all-purpose flour
- 1/2 cup grated Parmesan cheese

- 2 eggs, beaten
- Salt and pepper to taste
- 1/4 cup vegetable oil

Directions:

1. In a large bowl, combine the grated zucchini and onion.
2. Add the flour, Parmesan cheese, eggs, salt, and pepper. Mix well.
3. Set the vegetable oil in a skillet over medium-high heat to warm it up.
4. Scoop out tiny amounts of the zucchini mixture with a spoon and form them into patties.
5. Set the patties in the skillet with caution, and cook for 2-3 minutes on each side, or until golden brown.
6. Drain the patties on a paper towel to remove excess oil.
7. Serve the zucchini patties warm with your favorite dipping sauce.
8. Note: you can also add some herbs such as parsley, dill, or cilantro to the mix for extra flavor.

Nutrition: Calories: 245; Fat: 15g; Carbs: 16g; Protein: 13g

Sweet and Spicy Tofu Salad with Carrot

Preparation time: 30 minutes

Cooking time: 20 minutes

Ingredients:

- One block of firm tofu drained and pressed
- 2 tbsp soy sauce
- 1 tbsp rice vinegar
- 1 tbsp sesame oil
- 1 tsp sriracha (or more, to taste)
- Two medium carrots, grated
- Two green onions, thinly sliced
- 1 tbsp sesame seeds (optional)

Directions:

1. Divide the tofu into small cubes and set them aside.
2. Mix the soy sauce, rice vinegar, sesame oil, and sriracha in a small bowl to make the dressing.

3. Set a pan over medium-high heat to heat up. Once the pan is hot, add the tofu and cook for about 5 to 7 minutes, until it is golden brown.

4. Take away the tofu from the pan and set it to a large bowl.

5. Place the grated carrots, green onions, and sesame seeds (if using) to the dish with the tofu.

6. Pour the dressing over the tofu and vegetables and toss everything together until well coated.

7. Serve immediately, or chill in the refrigerator before serving.

Nutrition: Calories: 600; Fat: 0g; Carbs: 87g; Protein: 28g

Marinated Cucumber & Tomato Salad

Preparation time: 15 minutes   Cooking time: 120 minutes

Ingredients:

- 2 large cucumbers, skinned, halved, and thinly sliced
- 2 cups cherry tomatoes, divided
- 1/2 cup red onion, thinly chopped
- 1/4 cup sliced fresh parsley

- A quarter cup of white wine vinegar
- 2 tbsp. of olive oil
- 1 tbsp. honey
- 1 tsp. of Dijon mustard
- 1/2 tsp. salt
- 1/4 tsp. black pepper

Directions:

1. In a large bowl, combine the sliced cucumbers, cherry tomatoes, red onion, and chopped parsley.

2. In a small bowl, set together the white wine vinegar, olive oil, honey, Dijon mustard, salt, and black pepper.

3. Pour the dressing over the cucumber mixture and stir to coat.

4. Cover and put in the fridge for at least two hours and up to eight hours to let the flavors blend. Toss the salad before serving.

Nutrition: Calories: 90; Fat: 7g; Carbs: 6g; Protein: 1g

Wilted Spinach and Tilapia Salad

Preparation time: 20 minutes   Cooking time: 5 minutes

Ingredients:

- Four tilapia fillets
- Salt and pepper, to taste
- Two tablespoons olive oil
- 4 cups fresh spinach leaves
- 1/4 cup red onion, thinly sliced
- 1/4 cup cherry tomatoes, halved

- Two tablespoons lemon juice
- One tablespoon balsamic vinegar
- One tablespoon honey
- One clove garlic, minced
- 1/4 teaspoon Dijon mustard

Directions:

1. Add salt and pepper to the tilapia fillets.
2. Warmth one tablespoon of olive oil in a skillet over medium heat.
3. Set the tilapia fillets in the pan and cook them on each side until the fish is achieved.
4. Take out the tilapia from the pan and set it aside to cool.
5. Mix the spinach, red onion, and cherry tomatoes in a large bowl.
6. In a different dish, combine the lemon juice, balsamic vinegar, honey, garlic, and Dijon mustard.
7. Slowly drizzle the remaining one tablespoon of olive oil while constantly whisking to emulsify the dressing.
8. Set the sauce over the salad and toss to coat the greens evenly.
9. Flake the cooled tilapia into bite-sized pieces and add them to the salad.
10. Toss gently to combine, then serve.

Nutrition: Calories: 186; Fat: 9g; Carbs: 8g; Protein: 20g

30-DAY MEAL PLAN

DAY	BREAKFAST	LUNCH	DINNER	SALAD
1	Peanut Butter Banana Outmeal	Turkey and Spinach Rice Bowl	Pocket Eggs with Sesame Sauce	Marinated Cucumber & Tomato Salad
	pg.15	*pg.34*	*pg.71*	*pg.120*
2	Muesli with Raspberries	Pesto Pasta	Lentil Walnut Burgers	Avocado and Eggs Salad
	pg.27	*pg.62*	*pg.72*	*pg.116*
3	Pistachio & Peach Toast	Shrimp Scampi with Zoodles	Lemon-Thyme Chicken	Salad of Kale, Avocado, and Carrots
	pg.23	*pg.57*	*pg.92*	*pg.114*
4	Spinach Omelet	Rainbow Trout Baked in Foil	Broccoli and Gold Potato Soup	Fruit Punch Salad
	pg.12	*pg.54*	*pg.88*	*pg.115*
5	Bagel Avocado Toast	Broiled Tuna Steaks with Lime	Cauliflower Fried Rice	Spinach, Pears and Cranberries Salad
	pg.21	*pg.58*	*pg.82*	*pg.118*
6	Carrot Baked Oatmeal	Bourbon Steak	Mushroom Frittata	Zucchini Patties
	pg.20	*pg.43*	*pg.78*	*pg.118*
7	Shrimp salad with avocado	Maple Salmon	Zucchini "Spaghetti" with Almond Pesto	Tofu Salad
	pg.15	*pg.45*	*pg.73*	*pg.112*

8	Lentil Asparagus Omelet	Green Beans and Mushrooms Spaghetti	Chicken Kebabs	Potato Dumplings
	pg.13	*pg.51*	*pg.68*	*pg.110*
9	Breakfast Parfait	Sesame-Crusted Tuna Steaks	Acorn Squash Stuffed with White Beans	Sweet and Spicy Tofu Salad with Carrots
	pg.25	*pg.55*	*pg.90*	*pg.119*
10	Healthy Bread Pudding	Easy Keto Korean Beef with Cauli Rice	Portobello Mushroom with Mozzarella	Fruit Punch Salad
	pg.26	*pg.39*	*pg.67*	*pg.115*
11	Cannellini Bean & Herbed Ricotta Toast	Turkey Sandwich	Indian Spiced Cauliflower Fried Rice	Wilted Spinach and Tilapia Salad
	pg.28	*pg.52*	*pg.69*	*pg.121*
12	Summer Berry Parfait with Yogurt	Black Bean Risotto	Seared Tilapia with Spiralized Zucchini	Tofu Salad
	pg.32	*pg.49*	*pg.87*	*pg.112*
13	Egg Tartine	Chicken Kebabs Mexicana	Salmon with Creamy Feta Cucumbers	Roasted New Red Potatoes
	pg.28	*pg.63*	*pg.83*	*pg.110*
14	Strawberry Peach Smoothie	Lemon Garlic Mackerel	Spring Minestrone Soup	Fruit Punch Salad
	pg.25	*pg.58*	*pg.91*	*pg.115*
15	Peanut Butter Banana Oatmeal	Two-Mushroom Barley Soup	Chicken Satay	Roasted New Red Potatoes
	pg.15	*pg.35*	*pg.97*	*pg.110*

16	Raspberry Mousse	Fish Chowder Sheet Pan Bake	Grilled Squash Garlic Bread	Avocado and Eggs Salad
	pg.31	*pg.44*	*pg.80*	*pg.116*
17	Tofu Scramble	Chopped Power Salad with Chicken	Braised Cauliflower and Squash Penne	Creamy Quinoa, Lentils, and Vegetables
	pg.30	*pg.47*	*pg.77*	*pg.106*
18	Southwestern Waffle	Chicken Cutlets with Pineapple Rice	Tarragon Sweet Potato and Egg Skillet	Tomato Cucumber Salad
	pg.22	*pg.64*	*pg.75*	*pg.113*
19	Pineapple Grapefruit Detox Smoothie	Spaghetti Squash and Chickpea Sauté	Farro with Sun-Dried Tomatoes	Spinach, Pears, and Cranberries Salad
	pg.23	*pg.61*	*pg.74*	*pg.118*
20	Spinach & Egg Scramble with Raspberries	Maple Salmon	Tofu Vegetable Stir-Fry	Quinoa Spinach Power Salad
	pg.20	*pg.45*	*pg.70*	*pg.113*
21	Shrimp Salad with Avocado	Easy Keto Korean Beef with Cauli Rice	Salmon with Creamy Feta Cucumbers	Zucchini Patties Creamy
	pg.15	*pg.39*	*pg.83*	*pg.118*
22	Muesli with Raspberries	Fried Chicken Bowl	Creamy Chicken and Chickpea Salad	Loaded Sweet Potatoes
	pg.27	*pg.37*	*pg.87*	*pg.105*
23	Cannellini Bean & Herbed Ricotta Toast	Salmon and Summer Squash in Parchment	Simple Tomato Soup	Marinated Carrots Salad
	pg.28	*pg.53*	*pg.86*	*pg.111*

24	Bagel Avocado Toasts	Turkey and Spinach Rice Bowl	Lemon-Thyme Chicken	Tofu Salad
	pg.21	*pg.34*	*pg.92*	*pg.112*
25	Summer Berry Parfait with Yogurt	Chicken and Pesto Sourdough Sandwich	Mushroom Frittata	Potato Dumplings
	pg.32	*pg.34*	*pg.78*	*pg.110*
26	Coconut Milk Pudding	Pan-Seared Pork and Fried Tomato Salad	One Skillet Quinoa and Vegetable	Gingered Beef and Broccoli Salad Bowl
	pg.18	*pg.42*	*pg.74*	*pg.117*
27	Almond Butter & Roasted Grape Toast	Hawaiian Chop Steaks	Pocket Eggs with Sesame Sauce	Sweet and Spicy Tofu Salad with Carrot
	pg.26	*pg.45*	*pg.71*	*pg.119*
28	Carrot Baked Oatmeal	Black Bean Risotto	Tilapia with Tomatoes and Pepper Relish	Salad of Kale, Avocado, and Carrots
	pg.20	*pg.49*	*pg.85*	*pg.114*
29	Spinach & Egg Scramble with Raspberries	Grilled Chicken Breasts with Plum Salsa	Shrimp and Rice Noodle Salad	Quinoa Spinach Power Salad
	pg.20	*pg.62*	*pg.107*	*pg.113*
30	Egg Tartine	Oven Roasted Salmon Fillets	Creamy Quinoa, Lentils and Vegetables	Wilted Spinach and Tilapia Salad
30	*pg.28*	*pg.59*	*pg.106*	*pg.121*

Made in the USA
Middletown, DE
29 April 2023

29678815R00071